CHILDLESS BY CHOICE

MARIAN FAUX

CHILDLESS
BY CHOICE

Choosing Childlessness in the Eighties

ANCHOR PRESS/DOUBLEDAY
GARDEN CITY, NEW YORK

1984

Library of Congress Cataloging in Publication Data

Faux, Marian.
Childless by choice.

Includes bibliographical references and index.
1. Childlessness—Social aspects. I. Title.
HQ518.F38   1984   306.8′5
ISBN: 0-385-15845-9
Library of Congress Catalog Card Number: 83-2038

First Edition

For Rebecca Faux Swain

Preface

Like me, you may have noticed that there appear to be a lot of pregnant women about these days. Since you presumably were not in the middle of writing a book about childlessness, you may not have viewed these prospective mothers with quite the dismay I did. You would not have feared, as I did, that the women in their late thirties who had postponed having children had finally decided to have babies after all. I must confess it was with relief that I learned this was not the case, that the tide was not turning on the childlessness trend. Although some women in their late thirties and early forties who had delayed having children would make last-minute decisions to become mothers, many also would not. Some would try and fail, for prolonged ambivalence is a rather back-handed way of letting childlessness be the solution to one's ambivalence. What, then, accounted for this seeming epidemic of pregnant women? The answer was simple. A very large baby-boom generation, born during the post-World War II era, had come of age: there were a lot of women around of childbearing age, and many of those women—but far fewer than in preceding generations—were starting their families. My remaining fears that the option to be childless was merely a passing fad were further allayed when population expert Charles Westoff, head of Princeton University's Office of Population Research, predicted that as many as 25 percent of women now in their twenties will not bear children.

What I had suspected—what is the premise of this book—appeared to be true after all. An unusually high number of women are deciding not to have children. And childlessness has become an increasingly acceptable life-style.

What is really news, however, is not the fact that increased numbers of women are choosing childlessness, for these women will always be in the minority. Rather, it is the new ambivalence with which all women are viewing motherhood. It is probably safe to say that the possibility of childlessness now occurs at one time or another, however fleetingly for some, to almost every young woman, whereas a generation ago, it occurred to virtually no woman. If there had been no other substantial changes in women's lives over the past few decades, this attitudinal shift alone would be a major factor in the revolution that is currently under way in American family life.

In this book, I attempt to make a case for childlessness, to present the information that a woman examining the issues needs in order to make this very important decision. The fact that I have presented the antinatalist case so strongly is but an attempt to balance out the highly pronatalist view that prevails in our culture today. Despite this, I have not written this book as a polemic against motherhood, nor have I attempted to glorify childlessness, although it is something I avidly support for those women for whom it appears to be the right or the most comfortable decision.

I do not believe that childlessness is a counterpoint to motherhood. I would not like to see childlessness used as yet another issue to divide women against themselves. I see no reason that childlessness should necessarily be viewed as the opposite of motherhood; rather, I prefer to think of childlessness and motherhood as different—but not differing—aspects of the same issue: women's right to reproductive freedom. I do believe, however, that childlessness has social, cultural, and political implications that cannot be ignored, and I have attempted to explore them in this book.

This book was developed from available research and through my own interviews with women. Of the research, I can only report that there was a scarcity of material with which to work. A childless couple, until recently, was not even considered a family by those who take surveys to measure the tone and temper of American life; they were so few in number as to be either considered inconsequential to survey results or they were deliberately ignored. Often prejudice was involved in the decision to ignore them, since

several of the large fertility studies conducted in the 1950s and
1960s appear to have had as an underlying motive the goal of
finding ways to encourage women to have children.

The largest body of research about childless women up to the
time of this writing was done by sociologist Jean Veevers, who interviewed approximately forty women who were childless by
choice. I eventually did in-depth interviews with forty-three
women who were either highly ambivalent about having children
or who had already decided in favor of childlessness. I also interviewed six women who were ambivalent mothers. Willing to discuss their fears and ambivalences with friends, they seemed, for the
most part, incapable of discussing them for the record. I sympa-
thized. I had another problem in finding older, childless women to
interview, even though nearly every young, ambivalent woman I
talked to raised the question of how she would feel twenty years
after her decision to remain childless. In a further attempt to answer this question, I have explored the meaning of motherhood
socially and culturally, to see what keys it may hold to why women
choose to mother and what it means when they do not choose to
mother. I did interview four childless women ranging in age from
fifty-six to eighty-three, but the results were not very fruitful for
reasons that are described in greater detail later in the book. In addition to the in-depth interviews, I received responses to ques-
tionnaires from about twenty more women, and I talked informally
with many friends, acquaintances, and colleagues about childlessness.

I originally planned to include interviews with couples and men,
but I quickly backed off from this idea. At this stage, there is so
much to say about women and childlessness that I declined to
make the subject even more unwieldy than it was by adding other
elements. As for men's views about childlessness and children, that
would fill another book—a task I shall leave to some other writer.

My goal in writing this book has been to provide an overall perspective that will help women sort out their ambivalent feelings
about motherhood. Often, I have approached my subject from the
point of view of what it would be like to be childless. I have also
attempted to present both the practical and the theoretical issues of
childlessness, as well as to include the ideas and opinions of women
who are caught in the throes of maternal ambivalence. I made a

deliberate decision, however, not to include formal case histories. I realize they are an easy means of identification for the reader, but I question their validity in any book meant for a lay audience, and I would especially fear that their inclusion would lead to an over-simplification of the issues that concern ambivalent women. There are common characteristics shared by many childless women, and I discuss these at length in Chapter 2, but I felt confirmed in my decision as my interviews and research revealed how highly individual women's attitudes are on this subject.

Finally, I feel I should tell you what prompted me to write this book. Although the idea was suggested to me by an editor who later declined to buy the book because he thought the subject was too controversial, it was an idea that attracted me from the beginning, for the simple reason that I was a woman seeking to resolve my personal feelings about the role, if any, that motherhood will play in my life.

New York City
November 1982

Acknowledgments

After more than three years of interviewing, researching, and writing this book, I am indebted to more persons than I can possibly name in this limited space, but I do wish to thank the following:

All the women who graciously consented to discuss with me their deepest feelings and thoughts about motherhood and childlessness; without them, there would have been no book.

I was also deeply influenced in my thinking by the works of two women: Linda Gordon, author of *Woman's Body, Woman's Right: A Social History of Birth Control in America*, and Nancy Chodorow, author of *The Reproduction of Mothering: Psychoanalysis and the Sociology of Gender*.

For their friendship and support, as well as the contribution of important ideas and thoughts that I have incorporated into this book, I thank, in no particular order, Sally Chapralis, Barbara Bean, Barbara Moore, Thomas Moore, Krysia Poray Goddu, Marilyn Miller, Sharon McIntosh, and Kathryn Stechert.

I also wish to thank Dominick Abel, my literary agent, for his sound advice and encouragement.

Special thanks go to my typist Judy Waggoner, whose keen editorial eye was, as usual, an important help to me.

I also wish to thank Bill Willig for his support and encouragement.

Contents

"That she bear children is not a woman's significance.
But that she bear herself,
that is her supreme and risky fate."

D. H. LAWRENCE

CHILDLESS BY CHOICE

1.
THE PHENOMENON
OF CHILDLESSNESS:
An Introduction

The idea that a woman might choose not to have children first sprang into public consciousness in 1969, when Stephanie Mills, valedictorian of her class at Mills College in California, startled many people by announcing her decision to remain childless. In her commencement speech, she said, "I am terribly saddened by the fact that the most humane thing for me to do is to have no children at all."[1]

Her simple words resounded in the public mind (and undoubtedly in many women's private thoughts); commentary appeared in the weekly newsmagazines and in daily newspapers around the country. Years later, Mills stood by her view, saying, "It's like the famous question about the chicken and the egg, which came first, the idealism or the personal desire? It's hard to say. I never thought about not having children until I wrote that speech, but I suspect the idea was simmering under my consciousness for a long time."

It seems that "the idea"—the notion that women might not need children to lead complete, fulfilled lives—had been simmering in many women's consciousness for some time. In 1971 Ellen Peck wrote a best-selling book entitled *The Baby Trap*, in which she elucidated the case for childlessness.[2] Once again, women were reminded, if of nothing else, that there was a decision to be made about motherhood, that they need not always structure their lives around motherhood. Whether or not to have children has increasingly been an issue in the lives of women of childbearing age in the late 1970s and early 1980s. Despite an apparent baby boom, which has been precipitated by the fact that an unusually large generation of women have reached childbearing age and not because women have once again decided to have lots of babies or by last-minute decisions on the part of women in their thirties to become mothers after all, women have come to think of motherhood as an option. Like so many of the rapidly changing social and sexual mores of this era, motherhood, once virtually a mandate, has become a matter of choice.

People once again sat up and took note in 1975 when columnist Ann Landers invited her readers to comment on whether they would have children if they could make the decision all over again. A whopping 70 percent of the 50,000 who responded said no, they would not choose to become parents again. The rewards were too few and the sacrifices too great. One forty-year-old woman told Ann Landers she had gone from being an "attractive, fulfilled career woman" to an "exhausted nervous wreck who misses her job and sees very little of her husband." A seventy-year-old woman wrote of her frustration with motherhood, noting that parenting held no rewards for her and her husband: "God knows we did our best, but we were failures as parents, and they are failures as people."[3] Admittedly, those who answered Ann Landers' call to discuss parenting were a biased group against parenthood, consisting, as they did, of persons who were disgruntled enough to pick up a pen and write a letter on the subject. Still, of the 50,000 who responded, 35,000 expressed unhappiness over having become parents.

Prior to these startling media events, experts displayed little interest in voluntarily childless women, mostly because few of them thought such women existed. The rare woman who could conceive and chose not to do so, and who had the courage to announce her decision (and such women *were* incredibly rare), was pitied or viewed as an oddity by those who knew her. Therapists and social scientists had another description for her: she was displaying aberrant social behavior.

And indeed for many years, the majority of married women did not consider childlessness because they did not feel that they had any decision to make about whether or not to have children. With almost no exceptions, any married woman who was physically capable of reproduction simply did so with virtually no forethought or sense that this might not be something she really wanted to do, let alone something that might not fit in with her life at that time or even permanently.

In an interview for this book, one forty-two-year-old mother of a seventeen-year-old daughter and a fifteen-year-old son reflected the feelings of most women of her age and era, when she unwittingly reviewed the chronology of her and so many other women's lives: "I graduated from college, worked for about a year, married the man I had dated in college, and then, as soon as we felt we could afford to do so, started a family. Having children wasn't something I thought about. It just seemed a natural part of marriage—of life. We never even discussed children except for very vague plans that when we bought a house, we would, of course, start a family. We started saving for a house, so I guess I just knew, when we had enough money for a down payment, that the next step was to get pregnant. But I never really thought about it."

Another woman, now forty-five years old and rare among her peers in the early 1960s in managing to combine marriage, motherhood, and a successful career as a real estate agent, commented: "Having children wasn't something anyone thought about. They just did it. Women were first of all mothers, then wives, I guess, and then my work was something I fit in when I had the time and energy. I worked hard, don't get me wrong, but I knew my priorities. I love my children, but I can now say that I didn't love being a mother. That was a very taboo subject in the 1960s. I always felt this pull—there were always other things I wanted to do. But I knew I would have to do them when I wasn't being a mother or after my children were grown. The idea of not having children never even occurred to me, although I think it would today. But then, women today take a lot of things for granted that women my age never considered."

Of the women prior to the 1970s who chose childlessness (and statistics indicate that there always have been such women, since the number of women who do not have children is frequently higher than the number of women who cannot physically bear children), they were hardly vocal about their decisions. But many women who were not technically sterile probably were only aware of their reluctance to mother on a subconscious level. That their childlessness might be rooted in some form of deep-seated maternal ambivalence was generally unapparent even to the women themselves, mostly because many of the sophisticated tests to measure fertility that are commonplace today did not even exist fifteen years ago. Many childless women had no way of assessing why they were childless. In addition, because people were a good deal less psychologically aware then than they are today, the notion of not having children because one did not really want them largely went unrecognized. Yet, therapists have long been aware that a woman's ability to conceive depends in part on her psychological willingness to do so. Everyone knows or knows of a couple who, upon discovering they could not have children, adopted a child, only to find themselves bearing a child within a couple of years.

*

Until recently, most women who did not have children thought they were unable to conceive; very few were able to admit, even to themselves years later, that they simply may not have wanted children. Because of this, few women in their late forties and older were interviewed for this book. Although attempts were made to interview them, these women rarely were able to perceive that they may, in fact, have maintained a hidden psychological agenda not to have children.

Typical of these women was one childless widow, now eighty-six, who recalled: "When I married my husband, we tried very hard to have children. Of course, we didn't know anything about birth control in those days, so I never did anything to protect myself. We just never had any children. I don't remember feeling especially bad about it, though. You see, at that time, when we were first married, we lived in Detroit. Since I had grown up in a small town, living in such a big city looked glamorous to me. Those were exciting times. We were able to travel a lot. I worked for a business publisher. We had lovely friends. We entertained a lot, and people were always asking us to visit them. We were very popular, and we had such a nice crowd to run around with. It was a wonderful life.

"Of course, I never had what you might call a 'career,' but my boss liked me a lot. I was given more and more responsibility. And I felt very important when it came to my work. I felt the same way about it, I think, that young women feel today about work. But children? Oh, yes, we wanted them. We just never had any."

In talking with women in their forties, fifties, and older who just "happened" to be childless, one cannot help but be struck by the fullness of their lives despite the absence of children in an era when a couple truly became a family only after they had children. In an age when the accepted role for women was largely that of homemaker, many of these women worked at jobs they thoroughly enjoyed; many had active social lives; and many of their marriages retained a special vitality and closeness that sociologists have come to associate with the marriages of childless couples. It is impossible to say whether any number of these women "chose" childlessness, but the similarities of their lives and marriages to those of women and couples who today are consciously choosing childlessness cannot be lightly dismissed.

It was only in the 1960s, however, with the widespread use of the Pill and a renewal of interest in women's rights that women became fully aware that they could choose whether or not they wanted to be mothers and then act on that choice. With this possibility came a new kind of maternal ambivalence. Instead of emerging with often frightening suddenness after the birth of a child, maternal ambivalence was being experienced by women for several years while they were deciding whether or not they wanted to be mothers.

For most women, maternal ambivalence took the form of postponing marriage and children so they could devote their time and energy to their work. Family life would come later. A prevailing pattern in a young woman's life in the late 1970s and early 1980s has been for her to take a few years to establish herself in a career before taking "time off" for motherhood.

But as women have become more involved in careers that are demanding and challenging, the possibility of not having any children at all has become stronger. Although the number of women who will opt for childlessness is, and probably always will be, relatively small, the number of women who contemplate childlessness now includes almost every woman in her twenties, thirties, and early forties. In some circles, particularly in urban areas where other factors such as expensive housing and higher salaries for women play an important role in the decision to postpone children or even to remain childless, maternal ambivalence is an issue in a woman's life for a number of years, often as long as a decade or more. These women often subject themselves to several years of self-evaluation, evaluation of their marriages and their mates, and often quite painful soul-searching with regard to their careers before they are able to reach any decision.

The final results of the maternal ambivalence that has beset so many women today will not be apparent for many years, since any decision regarding children is viewed as an open-ended one by most women. It is what one woman referred to as "that nineteen-year decision."

Furthermore, the ambivalence deepens with age. Although many young women today believe that they intend to have children eventually and say they are only temporarily postponing them, the nature of this ambivalence is such that these women often delay until they can no longer have children. Their biological time clock has reached its deadline. In addition, the longer a woman delays children, the greater the chance that she will become so immersed in her career that she will be reluctant to take time out to have a baby; her life without children will become so comfortable that she will be less and less willing to make this major accommodation. While women have many options today that they did not have even twenty years ago, with so many choices for almost all women comes a heavy case of maternal ambivalence. Whether or not to have children is the predominant issue in the lives of many women of childbearing age today.

Only a generation ago, society's greatest reward was reserved for those women who devoted themselves entirely to motherhood. In the coming years, the biggest reward of all probably will be reserved for those women who manage to combine motherhood and a career successfully. For the present, however, combining these roles is extremely difficult and is a source of much of the maternal ambivalence women are experiencing. Whether some women will eventually be rewarded for remaining child-free remains to be seen, but on the most personal level, this choice has increasing appeal for young women.

Maternal ambivalence is nothing new, although until quite recently, it has mostly surfaced in women who were already mothers.

Collectively, women have always retained their (often unspoken) fears about their ability to shoulder the burdens of motherhood. Individual women have expressed their ambivalence in many ways, and not infrequently through acts of violence toward their children. Throughout history, while child abuse has been a crime perpetrated by both men and women, infanticide has almost always been the act of a desperate woman.[4]

But maternal ambivalence is always difficult to come to grips with, even in a time such as the present when women can talk freely about their feelings. Many women fail to see that, despite the difficulties inherent in confronting this issue, it is nonetheless something that they must come to grips with. Left unacknowledged, as just noted, maternal ambivalence can take an unhealthy and highly destructive turn that will have consequences for the woman, as well as for her child.

A woman grappling with maternal ambivalence has several courses of action open to her. The first step, of course, is to acknowledge the ambivalence. The next step is to attempt to examine it in its many contexts in order to figure out whether childlessness or motherhood is the best solution. She then needs to weigh how much support she will need and be likely to receive if she becomes a mother, as well as if she doesn't; how becoming a mother will change her life; and what her personal and professional life will be like with or without children.

Resolving the ambivalence is never easy, and many women never manage to tie up the loose ends. Some women have children and learn to live with their ambivalence toward them. Other women have children and find their lives, and often their children's lives as well, destroyed by their ambivalence. Other women do not have children and learn to cope with that, too. More often than in the past, though, women today are attempting to think through the issues so they can make a decision.

An increasing number of young women today find themselves comfortable with the possibility that they may never have children. They take their potential childlessness for granted the same ways their mothers took for granted the fact that they would become mothers.

Among women in their thirties and forties, those most troubled by maternal ambivalence, less is taken for granted. They remember when fewer opportunities existed for women, when women were expected to make children their careers. These women often began their professional lives with the full expectation that their careers would give way to motherhood. For women like this, there is a special jolt that comes from recognizing that the allure of a career is often a step away from motherhood—for many women of child-bearing age, it is the single biggest step.

Cynthia,* at age thirty-nine, was surprised to discover how much satisfaction she derived from her work. She was even more surprised to make the discovery that she might be leaning toward childlessness rather than forgo her career. "Somehow, I just thought I could manage everything—marriage, work, motherhood. And I guess I still maintain that I can. The issue now is, do I want to? I find my work as a lawyer very absorbing. And I was thirty-five when I graduated from law school, so I got a slow career start, like lots of other women my age who trained for one career and then decided on something more serious.

"I work for a large law firm where the competition is fierce. I shudder to think what would happen to me if I took any time off—even six weeks—to have a baby. I love my work, and my life is very full without a child, so I guess I'm in the process of deciding not to have one. My husband says it's okay with him."

Bobby, at forty, finds herself right up against her self-imposed deadline for deciding whether or not to have children. A child of the sixties, she somehow missed the marriage marathon being held in most colleges. After college she worked to carve out a successful career as a stockbroker, something that few women were doing at that time. She recalled: "I only got interested in work slowly. When I first got out of school, I thought I would work for a few years, settle down, and get married. I would have children, that was part of my master plan. This was before I figured out that I liked my work and was very involved in it.

"Actually, at first, it was touch and go. I worked long hours for a mere pittance. Gradually, though, I began to earn more money and got more responsibilities. That was when work became fun. It still is, and although I'm married now, I'm still not eager to have children because of my work. When I got married ten years ago, I would never have predicted that I would feel this way. It's just

* Pseudonyms have been used throughout this book.

something that happened to me. It may break up my marriage, but I simply cannot get enthusiastic about giving up everything I have to be a mother."

The lure of a career is probably the single most important factor drawing women toward childlessness. The common denominator among ambivalent women is often their dedication to their work. But as more women weigh the pros and cons of childlessness, as they develop a greater sense of shared concern over their inability to make a decision about motherhood, they naturally want to know more about other traits that childless and ambivalent women share. Are all voluntarily childless women alike? If so, how and to what extent? Do they form a readily identifiable group? Are such women selfish and antisocial, as some of their critics have maintained, or are they simply women who have a different agenda than those who become mothers? How successful are their childless lives? Their childless marriages?

Most important, women want to know whether they can expect to experience a sense of loss as a result of not having children. Are they denying something innate, and will there be a price to pay later, they wonder?

Childless women and women with deep-seated maternal ambivalence about children, a group that includes nearly all women today at one time or another, have begun to interest people other than themselves. The media, biologists, sociologists, economists, psychologists, psychiatrists, and demographers have all begun to take note of the effect that any change in the number of childless women could have in our culture. Mothers want to know what motivates their childless counterparts; men are intrigued by women who opt for a child-free life (and of course, many men share those feelings with women and wish to remain childless themselves). The most curious group, though, are the childless women themselves. They want to know who they are, how they got to be the way they are, and, most important, what the future holds for them. They, perhaps more than any other group of women, share a growing awareness of the myths that surround motherhood in particular and femininity in general, and they are eager to explore those myths so they can get on with the realities of their lives.

2.
WHAT KIND OF WOMAN DOESN'T WANT A CHILD, ANYWAY?

Despite the growing interest on the part of women themselves and also on the part of psychologists and sociologists in childlessness, little has been written about childless women. Journals and professional publications are curiously devoid of material about childless women; few books have been written on the subject. Of the material that exists, the names of the same researchers appear over and over again: the voluntarily childless, thus far, appear to have caught the attention of only a few experts and journalists.

For many years, in the eyes of many researchers, childless women and couples did not even exist. In books and journals about contemporary family life, families were often defined as consisting of parents and children—never as married, childless couples or, for that matter, as a group of adults living together, even if those adults happened to be related to one another.

Data on childless women are sorely lacking, even though several experts have drawn attention to the fact that research on childless women might lead to a greater understanding of parents. Ultimately, research on childless women could offer a key to understanding and resolving the issues that most women confront these days as they consider whether or not they want to be mothers.

For a long time, demographers and other researchers said they were unable to study childless women because they did not know where to look for them; they did not believe that any significant number of voluntarily childless women existed in our culture. That children would be part of every marriage, when possible, was an assumption rooted in the Judeo-Christian religion, and a widely held cultural belief stated that the primary purpose of families was to provide support and protection for children.

Some social scientists say they have avoided research about voluntarily childless women because of the problems in separating the real reasons from the rationalizations women give for childlessness. They point out that women who do not want children, for example, because of a fear about what the child will do to their sexual lives or because of a fear of pregnancy and childbirth, if asked, tend to offer more socially acceptable reasons such as cost or a strong career interest. Social scientists also feel that voluntarily childless women have a tendency to decide to remain childless and then develop their reasons *ex post facto* to support their decisions. This process of rationalization typically goes on in many people over important life-changing decisions. Yet, whether such reasons are rationalizations or realistic reasons for remaining childless, they still have a validity to the degree that they are part of any realistic portrait of voluntarily childless women.

A more subversive reason that voluntarily childless women have not been studied as extensively as they should have been undoubtedly centers on societal prejudice against justifying their existence or providing them with a more positive image than they now enjoy. Voluntarily childless women have often been depicted as selfish and even neurotic. To some extent this remains their popular image, despite the fact that population expert Edward Pohlman could find no evidence that childlessness was related to emotional or mental abnormality.[1] Unfortunately, the more prevalent cultural view remains that of psychoanalyst Erik Erikson, who wrote that the "woman who does not fulfill her innate need to fill her 'inner space,' or uterus, with embryonic tissue is likely to be frustrated or neurotic."[2] In 1979, in a speech given to 2,300 psychoanalysts at the Thirty-first International Psychoanalytical Association Congress in New York, Erikson reiterated his belief and issued a warning about the dangers of the trend toward fewer children. Childlessness represented, he said, "a real danger that a new kind of repression may become a mark of adult life."[3]

The result of the lack of research about voluntarily childless women is that the myths—that childless women are selfish, that childless women care only about material things, that childless women dislike children—persist or are misinterpreted in the face of so few hard facts to explain the phenomenon of voluntarily childless women. People ask themselves, What kind of woman doesn't want to have a child? And then people make up stories to supply themselves with an answer.

A Statistical Overview

Sociologist Jean Veevers was one of the first persons to attempt to find out what kind of woman remains childless voluntarily, how women evolve into childlessness, and what consequences, if any, their decision holds for them. By interviewing forty-two women in the late 1960s on the subject of voluntary childlessness, she conducted one of the largest surveys ever done. In 1976 Carl Lichtman wrote a dissertation at Columbia University Teachers College in which he attempted to establish a correlation between Veevers's and his findings. He interviewed twenty voluntarily childless couples. Men and women were interviewed separately. In addition, forty-nine women were interviewed in depth and many more contributed to this book less formally. The information that follows is mostly drawn from these sources and also from other, smaller studies.

Childless women tend to be urban, white, and well educated, facts that should surprise no one since most social change is initiated by persons with the education, time, and financial wherewithal to sustain them; new attitudes then filter down to the middle and lower classes, often after the ideas have first been made more palatable. In the Lichtman study, for example, the average combined income of husband and wife was $30,000 and the lowest was $11,800, with the next two highest incomes at $17,000 and $17,500, respectively. Five of the women had completed their educations at the high school level; eight had college degrees; and seven—an unusually high number—had professional degrees.[4]

The Childhoods of Childless Women

Of the small amount of research that exists on how a woman's childhood and family life may influence her desire to have children, the most salient finding is that the desire may not be based so much on what actually happened as on what was perceived to have happened. While no study has been undertaken of the childhoods of childless women as a contributing factor in the decision to remain childless, Veevers did suggest that "atypical" childhood experiences might figure in as a factor.[5] Proof that this is the case would be a substantial addition to the growing body of evidence suggesting that maternal love is learned rather than biological.

Lichtman, on the other hand, asked many questions about the childhoods of his subjects. He uncovered a range of experiences that varied from those who had been abused as children to those with normal childhoods to several persons who had received an excessive amount of parenting.[6]

Lee Hersh, another researcher, found that the marital status of one's parents made no difference in the decision to remain childless, although he did find that voluntarily childless couples were characteristically higher than their parents in income, education, and occupational status.[7]

Lichtman's findings and the interviews done for this book do suggest that childless women may share a perception of childhood that has somehow predisposed them toward childlessness. For example, many childless women believed their parents had been limited by the chores of parenting. They saw their parents as having limited their travel, careers, and mobility with regard to jobs for the sake of their children, and they were especially aware of the financial sacrifices they felt their parents had made to have children.[8]

In an interview for this book, Casey, a professional photographer who at thirty-seven has made the decision to remain childless, recalled her father's feelings about what he had done for his children: "I think his life was restricted by his children. He worked at a job for thirty-five years without ever complaining about it, but the day he quit, he told me that he had hated the job for thirty-four of the thirty-five years but had no other way of earning a living. He did it so he could raise a family and send kids to college."

Jeanette, thirty-six, a journalist who is ambivalent about whether or not to have children, admitted to having been influenced by her mother's attitudes about money. She said, "I try to remember she's a product of the Depression, and that she's always worried about money, but I also felt she underwent a real tug-of-war over spending money on her children. Sometimes she would be incredibly generous. I remember a couple of times when I was a teenager and she took me and my sister to a store and bought each of us $150 worth of underwear. Girls' underwear, nothing fancy, just a good supply that would last awhile. But then, there were a couple of years—when I was in eighth grade or ninth grade, I think—when she made all our school clothes, and I had very few things to wear. I had just two or three skirts, as I recall—few enough so that I felt awkward about it. We weren't poor, either, so I didn't quite understand it. Anyway, from all those ups and downs, I've been left with a fear that I would hate making sacrifices to have children, or that maybe I would be too selfish and not giving enough."

Another woman reported that her mother had suggested several times that her father would have started his own business had it not been for his responsibilities to his children. Instead, he spent thirty-odd mostly unhappy years at the same job, working for an insurance company.

One woman, who was able to decide to have a child only at the age of forty-one, admitted that she let similar frustrations stand in her way. She said, "My mother always gave me the impression that my father would have been a doctor had my brother and I not come along. Instead, he sold medical textbooks. My brother was not very smart, so the task of becoming a doctor fell to me. I studied premed all the way through college, then threw it all over at the last minute to become a secretary. That was, I now understand, about the most offensive thing I could do to my parents. I finally succumbed, for lack of a better word, to having a child because my husband pressured me into it. I became very depressed after I gave birth, so much so that I had to go into therapy. Gradually, I understood that I had a great deal of unresolved ambivalence about becoming a mother, that my mother had painted a bleak picture of parental sacrifice, and that I had believed it and been unable to shake it. Now I understand my ambivalence, but I don't think I'll ever shake it entirely."

In all fairness to those women who do parent, such sacrifices as less travel, less job mobility, and less career flexibility are acceptable trade-offs for the rewards of parenting. Some parents do not think of these trade-offs as sacrifices; of those who do, most would not live their lives any other way.

Another possibility is that childless women perceive these sacrifices as having been more meaningful or more overwhelming than their parents did. It may be that while all parents make some sacrifices for their children, some children may feel the burden of those sacrifices more acutely than others, and those may be the ones who are most likely either to feel that childlessness is right for them or to become mired in ambivalence.

Family Position and the Desire to Remain Childless

Among the women Lichtman interviewed, the woman's position in the family made little difference to her desire not to have children, but again, her perceptions regarding her familial position may have been relevant. Lichtman wrote: "Some respondents viewed their childhood in terms of a rivalry struggle with other siblings. As a result, their childhood was experienced as painful and viewed as limiting one's choices and inhibiting personal freedom and growth. They [the respondents] all noted in some way the 'free' feelings they now have in working and being independent. A child was seen as making them in a sense relive their painful childhoods and also inhibit [sic] their feeling of freedom."[9]

Many experts speculate that women who were burdened with the care of younger siblings, either because of the illness or death of their own mothers, are more likely to forgo having children of their own. Indeed, several of the women interviewed for this book expressed the sentiment that they had done enough parenting in their childhoods so that they did not want children of their own. Never having experienced particularly carefree youths, such women often appear determined to create one in their adult lives. One thirty-one-year-old woman said of her experience as the oldest of eleven children, "I already was a mother. I don't need to do that again." Many of the women interviewed, though, who had baby-sat frequently and had cared for younger siblings, felt this had little bearing on their decision not to parent. If anything, these women felt they had a more realistic picture of motherhood than others did and that they might make better mothers for having had the experience.

Sometimes, sibling rivalry is the motivating factor in voluntary childlessness, although again, the perception of what happened may be more important than the reality. One woman admitted that a fierce sibling rivalry with a younger sister probably contributed to her decision not to mother. She said, "I felt my parents' time was always divided, that I never got any personal attention. I know they were trying to be fair, so whatever they did for her, they did for me. If she got something in pink for Christmas, I got it in blue. If my mother spent an evening with me, she was very careful to balance it with an evening with my sister. But usually, we were viewed as a group, and I always felt it was an effort, a very deliberate attempt on my mother's part especially. I must admit that I now bask in being the sole center of attention where my husband is concerned."

Veevers found that a number of respondents were only children, and using their own self-reports of having been too much the center of their parents' attention, she speculated that this may have influenced their decision not to parent. This does not explain, however, why so many only children go on to become the parents of several children, but again, this may be related not to the facts of one's childhood but to one's individual perception of childhood.[10]

The Importance of Mothers as Role Models

A theme expressed repeatedly by childless women was that their own mothers had longed for careers they never had or had been forced to cut short their careers when they became mothers. All the women Lichtman talked to had nonworking mothers, and the majority of women interviewed for this book had mothers who either did not work outside the home at all or did not until the children were almost grown. This finding is interesting in light of recent research showing that many women today who successfully combine careers and motherhood had working mothers.

Lois Wladis Hoffman, who has done extensive research on working mothers, has noted that having a working mother tends to create an image of women that is less restrictive than when the mother's primary occupation is housework. The child of a working mother sees women in a wider range of activities. She develops, Hoffman wrote, "a self-concept that incorporates these aspects of the female role."[11] Women who had working mothers tend to view themselves as more competent and more capable of taking on multiple roles than do women who did not have working mothers.

In other research Grace Baruch and Lois Hoffman in separate studies found that the daughters of working mothers tended to list their working mothers as role models more often than did the daughters of nonworking mothers.[12] Cynthia Epstein, professor of sociology at Queens College and the Graduate Center of the City University of New York and an expert on women's roles, said, "I think that successful women often had mothers who did something. They may not have done the thing that this woman does, they may not even have worked, but they tended to be doers. Or they weren't defined as working, but somehow, they helped the father run the business. Some of the earlier women I interviewed had mothers who had been suffragettes. I think they had the experience of having had mothers who were effective."

Epstein also believes that successful career women in some way perceived during childhood that they were special or destined to do some special work. She notes that such women often were the eldest or the youngest child, or they were the child who survived in a family where several children died in infancy or were lost through miscarriage or stillbirth. "In other words," she noted, "they're identified as being special by their family in one way or another."[13]

Such women, it would seem, also perceive that they can handle a career and motherhood. Childless women, in contrast, viewing their mothers' frustration over not having careers, may have formed a perception that juggling motherhood and a career was simply not possible.

Casey saw her mother this way: "She was really a good mother and did all the right things—sewed and baked and took good care of the house—but I think she hated it all the time she was doing it. She went to work for the first time eleven years ago, and I would say, in ten years, that she hasn't cooked a meal, doesn't clean her house, even if she can get a maid, she won't do it. I don't think my mother liked being a housewife because she doesn't do it anymore."

Deborah's mother was not so frustrated, but she may have contributed to the same pattern in her daughter. At age forty, a successful business consultant, Deborah says, "I did see my mother combine meaningful work, if not a career, with housework, so I knew I had an option. She did make a big deal, however, of the career she had before she was married. She was proud of having worked before she was married."

A few of the women interviewed for this book said that taking care of a childlike, excessively dependent mother had influenced them against motherhood. One woman described how having a dependent mother had contributed to her own ambivalence: "My mother unloaded on me from the time I was old enough to listen. I not only felt I had to take care of her, but I felt afraid of how dependent she was on me, on my father, on everyone. It has taken me a long time to be willing to form a mutually dependent relationship with a man, and frankly, I just don't know whether or not I'm going to work through all the emotional problems connected with this in time to have a child. I still get panicked at the thought of someone depending on me utterly—and that's what a child does for a long time."

The Careers of Voluntarily Childless Women

Attitudes of voluntarily childless women about their work also reflect the fact that the message they got—or perceived themselves as receiving—from their own mothers was one of how difficult it is to combine motherhood and work outside the home. Voluntarily childless women seem to have quite willingly opted for careers, and they often view careers and motherhood as either/or situations, a finding that was first noted by Veevers.[14] As much as they viewed their careers as a full-time commitment, they also thought that children should be a full-time commitment, too. Many voluntarily childless women, in fact, were disparaging of feminism because they thought it placed too much emphasis on combining motherhood and work, which they often felt was impossible. Both Veevers's and Lichtman's subjects reported this antifeminist bias, but the more recent interviews done for this book reveal that while many voluntarily childless women consider themselves feminists, they think feminism has had little influence on their decisions to remain childless.

Jennifer, twenty-nine and a painter, expressed the view that she could not handle both her burgeoning career as an artist and motherhood: "I get aggravated when people tell me how easy having children should be for me since I work at home. I'm very driven about my work, and the last thing I would want is interruptions from some little person. On the other hand, if I were a mother—which I would only do if I could afford to have a housekeeper—and if I heard my child screaming or crying about something in some other part of the house, I know it would be hard not to stop work and go comfort that child. I've said I would move my studio out of the house the day I had a child, but I still think it would be hard to juggle everything. What happens when the child is sick or the housekeeper doesn't show up, or she quits when I'm trying to finish an important project? I just feel this tremendous conflict, and I think it's based on reality. I know how hard it is to do both things, so I'm only going to do one."

Deborah felt only slightly less strong about the conflict between motherhood and a career, when she said, "I always felt that I could continue my work at home if I had a child, so I never thought in terms of a child's ruining a career, but I do think that it would be very hard physically for me to do both. It's hard to work all day and come home and take care of a child."

All the voluntarily childless women felt that they were more free to pursue their work than were working mothers. They felt they had more mobility when their careers required it and more time to take on challenging work. They believed they took career risks that they would not be able to take if they were dividing their time between a career and motherhood.

The Marital Relationships of Childless Women

If voluntarily childless women are heavily involved in their careers, they are perhaps even more involved in their marriages. Veevers commented that voluntarily childless women tended to have strong marital relationships.[15] Of special importance to childless women and their spouses were the lives they were able to lead because they were childless. This feeling was also shared by single, voluntarily childless women. Both groups valued the unpredictability of their lives, the luxury of having no set routine, the opportunity to pursue unusual activities, and the opportunity to travel —all things these women felt were possible only because they were childless.

Lichtman noted, however, that only a few of the couples he interviewed actually took advantage of the freedom they described.
Many couples, for example, had only two weeks of annual vacation,
and they were often unable to schedule their vacations so they
completely overlapped. What mattered, then, to these couples was
their perception of being more free than parents were.

Researchers have found that religion played almost no role in the
lives of voluntarily childless couples, although Lichtman noted that
an unusually high number—eleven out of twenty—of the couples
he interviewed had married outside their religions.[16]

Lichtman also found that childless couples viewed children as a
financial burden,[17] although most of the women interviewed for
this book felt that the cost of rearing a child was not an important
factor in their decisions to remain childless. This difference may be
a result of the time that has elapsed between the two sets of interviews, Lichtman's having been done in the mid-1970s and the interviews for this book having been done in 1980 when many two-
career couples were enjoying unprecedented financial success. (See
Chapter 4, where this is discussed at greater length.)

The strides that women have made economically in the past decade have undoubtedly contributed to a greater sense that they can
afford children if they want them. In my interviews, many voluntarily childless women brushed aside the notion that cost would
matter to them, which was either an indication of the lack of reality with which they viewed the financial responsibilities attached to
parenting or a sign that, even in inflationary times, women today
feel more competent than women of previous decades to support
children because of the boost their salaries give to the family income.

Typical of the dismissal of the subject of the cost of children
were three comments by well-established businesswomen, all of
whom were earning between $20,000 and $40,000. One woman
said, "I'm not at all worried about money." Another said that the
cost of having a child simply did not worry her, although she con-
ceded that this might be a straw man because she had already decided not to become a mother. A third woman said, "I would be
able to afford good schools and full-time help so money just
wouldn't be a concern if I were thinking about becoming a mother.

I earn good money, and I probably would not marry someone who did not earn a lot, too. That's why money wouldn't be an issue."

Many of the women expressed a need to work because of the financial independence it gave them from their husbands, and all the women interviewed for this book said they would continue working were they to have children.

Outside Support: Childless Women Say They Don't Need It

Voluntarily childless women share yet another interesting characteristic in that they are not joiners. This is true despite the fact that several organizations that offer the possibility of joining a support network have sprung up for childless couples in the past decade. Childless couples often pay dues to Planned Parenthood or the National Alliance for Optional Parenthood, but many expressed impatience with meetings and the time they took, a sign that they do not feel much need for this kind of formal support system.

The reason that voluntarily childless women do not take advantage of the few support systems that are available may reside in their marital relationships, which, as several researchers have noted, tend to be especially close—close enough, in fact, to be the cause of critical comment on the part of some who have studied them. Lichtman is typical of researchers who express reservations with this aspect of voluntarily childless couples' lives. Noting that the "my-spouse-is-my-best-friend" syndrome popped up repeatedly during his interviews, he felt that such couples maintained a level of intimacy that served to distance them from others, particularly couples their age who were parents. He found that most couples had divested themselves of their relationships with friends who became parents; the same pattern shows up in voluntarily childless women's reluctance to form friendships with women who are mothers.

Other experts see the tendency of these childless women not to associate with mothers as a healthy sign of self-acceptance. Cynthia Epstein, who is among those who take this view, commented, "People always seek out—they should seek out—others of like kind. People tend to do that, anyway. Their life situation provides them with that kind of opportunity. For those who don't, well, they are stacking the deck against themselves."[18]

She described how difficult, for example, living in the suburbs is for a working mother, a single woman, or a voluntarily childless woman: "A lot of women have stacked the deck against themselves by choosing to live in the suburbs, by choosing to live where other women don't work, things like that. Those are choices that create terrible problems, but other kinds of choices make those problems more solvable. I think the consequences of where one chooses to live are clear. Why do women do that to themselves? The cultural pressure with regard to status, the cultural emphasis on rearing children in a rural setting, is part of the American tradition—that's the reason working mothers end up in the suburbs."

Epstein believes that voluntarily childless couples do not deliberately seek out—and may deliberately avoid—couples with children, because they get more social support from seeking out their own kind, who mostly reside in urban areas. She added, "There is a lot more social support these days for people not to have children. It used to be considered absolutely reprehensible. Now other people can understand why people might not want to have children. I think part of the whole movement of a greater sense of individualization came out of the sixties and people's right to choose the kind of life they want to lead was the prologue for some of the decisions being made now."[19]

Do Childless Women Dislike Children?

Related to the fact that many voluntarily childless women choose not to befriend their peers who have children is the belief that childless women dislike children and women their age who are mothers. Veevers and Lichtman did find some support for this in their research.

Lichtman reported that his subjects displayed some negative views toward children and parents, stating that children were "cruel," "hostile," "demanding," "noisy," "untamed," and "vicious." His subjects reported that they only enjoyed children when they were "intelligent" or "intellectually oriented."[20] He also noted that childless women tended to be intolerant of working mothers. They voiced feelings that working mothers neglected their children and that many child-care facilities appeared to be inadequate.[21]

Veevers also found this negative element in voluntarily childless women's attitudes toward children and mothers, but she attributed it to the way in which some women arrive at the decision not to have children. Among those who postponed making a firm decision, she found little hostility toward mothers and children. Part of maintaining an image of normality, which, in turn, is made possible through postponing rather than definitely deciding to be childless, is accomplished through identifying with mothers and children; thus, there is little incentive to dislike either group. Women who make a definite decision in favor of childlessness, though, have a stake in maximizing the differences between themselves and mothers, i.e., between themselves as persons who dislike children and parents, who obviously like them. These women, Veevers found, tended to view motherhood as harmful, painful, and dangerous physically and psychologically and to distance themselves from children, mostly by announcing their dislike for them.[22]

The women interviewed for this book evinced no dislike for either children or mothers, although sometimes the mothers of small children were viewed as less interesting or attractive than career women, a bit of projection that is perhaps only natural. There was a recognition that voluntarily childless women were often more comfortable with each other, just as mothers tend to seek out one another.

Many of the women, like Jeanette, recognized that they had few, if any, mothers as friends: "I've noticed that I always used to have a friend or two who was a mother. I used to make a point of spending time with my friends' kids, too, when I was in my twenties. Those were often friends from college. I would baby-sit for the day, take the kids to the zoo or the circus, or some such activity. Now I do it less and less, although I'm not sure why. Well, for one thing, lots of those women and their children have moved to the suburbs, and that makes it much harder for us to get together. Most of my friends come through my work, and I just seem to know other working women who are not mothers. But I don't think it's deliberate on my part that I don't know lots of persons with children."

Deborah, who acknowledges that at age forty she is still too ambivalent to opt for sterilization, but who foresees that there is "realistically very little chance that I will have a child," not only does not dislike children but has put herself in active contact with them, by leading a Girl Scout troop and maintaining close friendships with the children of the man with whom she has lived off and on in the ten years since her divorce. She said, "I have always felt a very strong maternal drive. I watch children. I think I had a positive experience in rearing my sister. I was nine when she was born, and our relationship goes beyond that of sisters. I think it is more mother-daughter. I had a grandmother who was very nurturing, so I saw that, too. My family always talked about children, so I was conditioned to feel this way. I think that motherhood is one of those things that as a woman you can do, and I always want to do everything I can do. Sometimes it irritates me that I'm consciously not going to do something that I'm capable of doing, but I don't think it has anything to do with my femininity. I don't feel less feminine, but I do feel funny sometimes around mothers. There's a little bit of that notion that motherhood is some secret initiation rite. There is that feeling among mothers, of, well, we've been through it, and you haven't."

Casey, who spent a year when she was married trying to get pregnant and who was sterilized three years ago at the age of thirty-five, has always been nurturing toward the children of men she has been involved with. She still knows where she stands, though: "I think babies look cute for a few minutes, but that's it. I do have more friends who are childless. I also have a lot of friends who have grown children, but none with little ones. Not being part of a marriage for so long made me drift away from having married friends. I sort of wish one of my friends would get happily married and have kids so I could have some in my life, but I don't know anyone who's even close."

Possibly this lack of hostility or negative feelings toward mothers and children reflects a lessening of social pressure on women to have children, which, in turn, decreases the need for voluntarily childless women to display hostility toward mothers and children.

Feeling Stigmatized over Childlessness

Veevers reported that the women she interviewed felt stigmatized because of their decision not to have children.[23] Lichtman, on the other hand, found a lack of social pressure toward parenthood;

his subjects were not feeling stigmatized by their decision to remain voluntarily childless.[24]

One reason so many of Veevers's subjects felt stigmatized may have been the fact that she interviewed mostly rural and suburban women, as opposed to the mostly urban women in other research. Epstein has noted that childless women can protect themselves to a degree by living in an urban area, where they will not only find many persons who do not consider their decision to remain childless unusual, but also will find other women like themselves. Such women, as Lichtman recognized, may need the "liberal atmosphere, anonymity, and lack of community ties" that are part of big-city life.[25]

The lessening of the stigma associated with childlessness has also undoubtedly occurred because a decade of inflation has sent many women into the work force who were not there before 1960, and because of a growing awareness of the problems of overconsumption and overpopulation, all of which are making childlessness an increasingly acceptable choice.

Childlessness and a Healthy Self-image

The image of a childless woman has often been that of a person suffering from low self-esteem who is somewhat deficient in traditional feminine attributes. Certainly, it has been one of a woman who is too selfish to make the sacrifices that being a parent requires. Typical of the attitude expounded by those who fall into this conservative camp is that of psychologist Judith Bardwick, who wrote in 1971:

> In the reality of current socialization and expectations, I regard women who are not motivated to achieve the affiliative role with husband and children as not normal. . . . When these are absent, denied, defended against, my clinical observation is that there is evidence for pathological levels of anxiety, a distorted sex identity, and a neurotic solution.[26]

In one sense, this view, which is far less common today, should not be surprising, in view of the fact that many women who wanted to become mothers but were unable to do so sometimes tended to set themselves up as objects of pity. That this same image has carried over to women who do not want children even though they are perfectly capable of having them is not too surprising.

Fortunately, research does not tend to support this image of voluntarily childless women. In a recent study, Judith Teicholz compared two groups of women on the subject of childlessness. All the women were ages twenty-three to thirty-eight and in stable marriages. In one group, each of the women had made the decision to remain childless; the other group consisted of childless women who hoped to become mothers in the future. Teicholz found no significant differences, after extensive testing, in the women's levels of femininity, levels of neurosis, and degrees of socialization. The only discernible difference she found was that some voluntarily childless women tested as more androgenous than did the test group who wanted to be mothers.[27]

Other research has also supported the finding that aggressive women also tend to be more nurturing by society's standards of femininity than less aggressive women are. Veevers, for example, found that aggressive women were also "independently rated as more maternal, more attractive, and more competent in their sex roles than the more 'feminine' subjects."[28] These findings are not surprising in light of Teicholz's research showing that childless women are more androgenous than traditional women, since someone who is androgenous, by definition, would have strong characteristics of both males and females.

*

Before a woman can resolve her maternal ambivalence, she must ask herself many questions, and she must carefully weigh the life she will lead as a child-free woman against the life she would lead as a mother. Many of these questions she must answer are of a surprisingly practical nature. Does she have the kind of marriage that can accommodate the changes she will need to make if she has a child? How will her career be affected by having a child? What kind of support system, if any, can she count on if she opts for motherhood? How will she structure her life to accommodate childlessness? For example, will she want or need to seek out other ways to nurture, as Casey and Deborah did, or will she not feel this as a particular lack in her life?

More important, though, a woman who remains child-free ultimately needs the self-confidence to know that her decision was right for her. To achieve this, any woman contemplating childlessness must also examine the diverse social, cultural, and political pressures on her to become a mother, in order to understand what her rejection of those values means.

3.
CONSIDERING THE CHILDLESS MARRIAGE

Most women do not seriously consider having a child until they are ready to marry. And until recently, that a man and woman would have children when they married was taken for granted. Children were viewed as the natural products of a happy marriage, and even in a faltering one, there was the optimistic if somewhat naïve hope that they might hold the marriage together. The question, then, was never *if*, but rather, *when*. Any discussion that preceded the decision to have children focused on such matters as timing, cost, and housing, if indeed, there was any discussion at all.

Today, however, the focus of discussion about having children has shifted, and ambivalence about whether or not to have any at all is a chief topic of discussion among married couples. New questions are raised: How will a child change a woman's career path? Can she even afford to take time out from a demanding career to have a child? How will the marriage relationship change? What domestic arrangements would have to be made? Can she afford to keep her present life-style and have a child?

For many women, the change in the marriage relationship—and, by association, in their domestic lives—that would accompany the birth of a child is an important consideration. Typical of the feelings of many young professional women today is this comment by a thirty-four-year-old lawyer: "Not only am I frantically busy most of the time, but my husband works even harder than I do. I'm just not sure how children would fit into our marriage or if bringing a child into our hectic existence would even be fair. It wouldn't work right now—and maybe it won't ever work."

Others are more directly concerned with the emotional timbre of the relationship, as this woman's comments indicate: "My husband and I are so close that I frankly can't imagine anyone becoming part of our relationship." Another woman, when asked whether she and her husband had ever considered having children during their twelve-year-old marriage, replied, "Only a few months after we started dating, we couldn't imagine not having each other. We said to ourselves that someday we would feel the same way about a child. We just wouldn't be able to imagine not having one. Well, that has never happened. We've never felt that we couldn't live without a child, so we've never had one. We discuss it, but we've never felt ready to go ahead."

Ambivalence has not only become an important subject of discussion among women of childbearing age and their spouses, but also among sociologists, who have turned their attention to what happens to a marital relationship when a child is brought into it. What they have learned provides a better picture than has ever before been presented of the effects of childlessness, as well as the effects of children, on a marriage.

Children as a Crisis in Marriage

Until recently, the birth of a child typically followed so closely on the heels of the marriage ceremony that experts were unable to sort out the various effects of each event. When couples began to postpone children, and several years separated the time of marriage and the arrival of the first child, the differences between the two events could more easily be discerned.

One of the earliest and most prolific researchers in this field, E. E. LeMasters, was also one of the first persons to suggest that the introduction of a child into a marital relationship provoked a crisis, or trauma.[1]

There was initially, and continues to be, some resistance to labeling the birth of a child as a crisis. Many experts admit they have an optimistic bias, that is, a culturally induced tendency to want to view marriage and children as positively as possible. Even LeMasters questioned the use of the word "crisis" at one point.[2] Sociologist Alice Rossi, an authority on parenthood, expressed her dislike of the use of the word "crisis," saying she felt it connoted a pathology. Rossi eventually came to support the new emphasis on studying the effects of parenting on children even if it was referred to as a crisis because of her belief in Erik Erikson's theory that human personalities are unstable. He believes that personalities are constantly changing and that people do sometimes respond dramatically to a critical turning point in life such as becoming a parent.[3] In particular, a woman who has delayed motherhood for whatever reason, but especially because she needs time to work out psychological stumbling blocks to motherhood or serious conflicts between motherhood and her career, may have trouble in accepting motherhood and its overwhelming responsibility as anything less than a crisis.

But if crisis research is defined as the study of important or meaningful turning points in one's life, then giving birth, or, for that matter, not giving birth, fulfills the definition. Even more important is the fact that crisis research has precipitated a shift in focus from the effect a mother has on a child to the effect a child has on its mother. This, in turn, has led to discussion about what good parenting is and is not, two subjects of conjecture that have long baffled experts and parents alike. It has led to the study of previously untouched topics such as maternal deprivation, the effect of full-time motherhood on women's emotional health, and the ability of women to form close ties to their babies.

This research has had repercussions on children's lives, too. It especially has opened the door to questions about what can go wrong in the parent-child relationship, and this has contributed to greater understanding of the causes of child abuse. Child abusers are now viewed more sympathetically than they were in the past when less was known about them. Persons who are likely to have difficulty with parenting, often because they were themselves abused as children, can now be helped to decide either to remain childless or to obtain the support therapy they need to become successful parents.

But, of course, the most important result of crisis research for our purposes is the recognition it grants to maternal ambivalence. It acknowledges that it exists and that it may not be "cured" simply by having a baby—or, for that matter, by deciding not to have one. The issues are far more complex than was previously supposed, and experts now recognize that some women need support as they attempt to resolve their ambivalence.

Crisis research about parenting is based on the theory that a family is an integrated social system and that the introduction of a new member naturally leads to a reorganization of the system. Mostly, this concept is drawn from role-theory research, which suggests that disruption of affection and intimacy occurs whenever a dyad, or couple, becomes a triad, a couple with a child.

In his article "Parenthood as a Crisis," LeMasters's research on small groups found that a couple with a child tend to form a pair and an isolate rather than merging into one group. Sometimes the husband is the isolated person as he watches his wife direct her attention, which he formerly received, toward their child, and sometimes the wife is the isolated person, when, for example, her spouse appears to show more interest in their child than in her.[4]

LeMasters found that the effect of a child on a marriage was so pervasive that parenthood rather than marriage was the real "romantic complex" in American life. It and not marriage, in his eyes, was the event about which people maintained the greatest number of illusions.[5] The trauma of becoming a husband and wife was nothing compared to the trauma of becoming a parent, or so it seemed from his research.

LeMasters reported that couples he interviewed expressed anger and dismay over their lack of preparedness for their roles as parents. In one study, LeMasters found that thirty-eight of forty-six couples reported a "severe" crisis in adjusting to the birth of their first child, despite the fact that thirty-five of the thirty-eight couples said they had wanted the child, and thirty-four of the thirty-eight marriages were considered happy.

LeMasters also ascertained that the crisis was not the result of a neurotic reaction to giving birth. Mothers described the crisis as resulting from a combination of factors that included loss of sleep, constant exhaustion, extensive confinement to home, curtailment of social contacts, loss of extra income, guilt at not being a "better" mother, and worry about physical appearance—the same concerns that ambivalent women raise over and over again in conversation with one another and with women who are mothers. In LeMasters's research, the number of couples who did not experience parenthood as a crisis was so small that no generalizations could be made

about them.[6] Other researchers have found that the group that experienced the highest level of crisis were middle-class people—the
very group that spends most of its time today grappling with their
ambivalence.

It is not very difficult to see why the birth of a child would precipitate a marital crisis. Rossi, in her article "Transition to Parenthood," pays special attention to the factors that make parenthood
so disruptive.[7] In part, the disruption occurs, she notes, because
there are so many unpredictable elements in parenting, elements
that haunt even the most highly motivated and unambivalent of
prospective parents. Before you have a child, for example, you can
know little about what it will be like, or even whether it will be
healthy. By comparison, you can, if you choose to do so, learn a
great deal about a prospective mate, a new job, or a city you are
considering moving to. With few exceptions, though, there is no
way to predict a child's personality, temperament, and intelligence
prior to its birth.

Some women, particularly those who are eager to be mothers, accept these unknowns with equanimity. For a woman who is ambivalent, though, the uncertainty can loom large. And for the
woman who has postponed motherhood into her late thirties or
early forties, there is another burden, since her chances of having
a physically or mentally handicapped child increase with age. Many
women expressed fears about this and said their fears only grew
as they got older and found themselves still ambivalent.

One woman, now forty-one and in what she considers a period of
"final review" regarding whether or not she will have a child, said,
"When I was younger, I think I was more willing to accept the fact
that I might have a less than perfect child. Now, quite frankly, I
find that idea hard to cope with, mostly for a very practical reason.
I'm very tied to my work, and I can only visualize having a child if
I can continue working. A handicapped child would obviously
change everything. I would feel that I had to stay home to take
care of such a child, and I also know how expensive caring for the
handicapped is. This is what always scares me away when I get
ready to have a child."

Another woman, age twenty-four, commented, "I'm something of
a perfectionist, and I honestly don't know if I could handle having

a handicapped child. I don't admit it to everyone, but that's how I feel."

Unfortunately, there is no easy way to resolve these fears, so strong in ambivalent women. Women with these fears need to recognize that they cannot rehearse for motherhood in any way that is comparable to the way that one prepares for work through education or special training or for marriage by dating. Compared to a new job, where you can beg off certain responsibilities until you feel ready to handle them, most new mothers have no one with whom to share their responsibilities for most of the day. They are totally responsible for the care of another human being—often for the first time in their lives.

And unlike an unsatisfying job or a miserable marriage, which you can choose to end, there is no clear-cut end to parenting. Parental responsibilities may end when your child finishes high school, or they may become considerably heavier because your child enters college. Even completion of education does not guarantee the end of a parent's emotional or financial responsibilities, since in our culture, there is no set time for a child to leave its parents' care.

If the end of parenting drags on, the beginning is frighteningly abrupt. There is no transition period, and parents caught up in caring for their first child often suffer from their lack of preparedness for this new role. Often, turning to the experts offers little consolation or real help; experts do not agree, and every parent has felt some despair over how little is really known about how to parent successfully.

The changes brought about by parenthood are not so unmeasurable or so ephemeral that they cannot be examined. A couple can, in many ways, consider and evaluate what will happen to their lives and their relationship if they decide to have a child.

Expectations About Parenthood

With great perception, childless couples often joke that they would have to "grow up" if they had children. While "growing up" may not be the most accurate description of what can happen to a marriage when a child is born, people are right to sense that major adjustments will be required of them. In general, the biggest changes will occur in a couple's financial, sexual, and interpersonal relationships.

The Financial Changes

Many of the ambivalent women interviewed for this book felt that rearrangement of their financial priorities would not be a major problem for them if they decided to have a child. Nor was the cost of a child seen as a heavy burden. All these women did, however, mention their comfortable to highly lavish life-styles with some pride, and most indicated they would not like to lower their standard of living to have a child.

One woman, expressing the certitude of many others, commented, "I would be able to afford a full-time housekeeper, so I cannot imagine that money would ever be an issue for me. The housekeeper would also mean that I would be free to continue to do the things I now enjoy—tennis, dining out with my husband, getting away for the weekend."

A few women managed a more realistic view of the financial adjustments that would have to be made. One woman commented, "I earn a very good living, and so does my husband, but I still shudder when I think how much more we would have to spend to have a child. Housing is sky-high, and I've been told that housekeepers or nannies cost a minimum of $10,000 a year. Sometimes, we shake our heads and joke that it is possible for a family to have an income of $60,000 a year these days and still be poor."

For many couples, the financial costs of having a child (which are examined in Chapter 4 in greater detail) are not as much of a problem as the shifts in spending patterns and the conflicts that result. Changes in spending patterns can be especially hard on couples who previously have been able to afford anything they wanted and who have often formed the habit of rewarding themselves and each other with lavish gifts of the kind that a parent often gives a child. This indulgence is common and frequently mentioned by couples who are ambivalent about children.

One woman said, "I think we take care of each other so well because we are trying to re-create childhoods that were not particularly pleasant for either of us. It's part of our ambivalence about having children." She added, "We are not especially materialistic. For example, we have been very slow about fixing up our house. But we do both love to travel, and we spend a great deal of money on that every year. It's our great passion and pleasure, and I know it's incompatible in many ways with having a family."

When a baby arrives, couples do find themselves facing new kinds of financial problems—how to afford a larger house or apartment, how to pay more bills (often with less money coming in), and how to give up luxuries that have begun to feel like necessities. Suddenly, a savings account that previously would have been used for a European holiday or a fur coat is cleaned out to pay for a house, a car, or medical bills.

Often conflict surfaces over money, even among couples who have never fought over it before. The expenses may be unavoidable, but the frustration of spending money in this way creates a new tension within the marriage. In one study, *The Quality of American Life,* by Angus Campbell and others, in which none of the participants had unusually high incomes, childless couples reported feeling happier with their savings and less worried in general about paying their bills than did couples with a child under the age of six.[8]

Conflicts over how money is spent also do not necessarily resolve themselves after a child is born; more often they continue for as long as the parents support the child. Over half of all couples with a child under age six reported disagreements with their spouses over money. Couples rearing children say their primary worry is money.[9] And almost all parents report making some financial sacrifices, often long-term ones. One researcher reported: "Most parents postpone major undertakings, such as a long vacation or refurbishing their home or acquiring a summer place and other comforts, until the departure of children."[10]

Too, often, couples focus on whether or not they can afford to have a child rather than on whether their marriage can afford the strain that is likely to result from making dramatic changes in spending patterns. If the bottom line looks right, they think they are ready to go ahead. Frequently, these couples are only setting themselves up for later conflict.

Ironically, there may be a grain of truth to the belief that people should have children whether or not they can afford them. If a couple truly wants a child, they will be less likely to resent lowering their standard of living, sacrificing luxuries, or choosing which necessities will be purchased. But a couple who have structured their marriage around their own idiosyncratic and often lavish spending patterns, who, in short, have acquired a taste for activities and possessions that may not be so feasible—either financially or logistically—after a child is born, may have created a relationship that will be unable to stand the strain of adding a child. One possible test is to practice making the shifts that will be required in spending patterns before deciding to have a child. If there is resentment over putting money in a savings account to pay for a baby rather than going to Europe or buying a new car, then perhaps the time is not right to have a child—and it may never be. As much as possible, a couple should try to resolve their difficulties over money before having a child.

The Sexual Changes

The second area where changes can be anticipated as a result of becoming parents is in a couple's sexual life. Many women express fears that a child may change their sexual lives. Almost all couples do report a change in their sexual relationships after the birth of a child, although whether or not the old spontaneity is regained, as it is in many marriages, depends on the individuals. Some couples with children still find ways to spend time with each other, although one thing is certain: with a child in the home, they have to work harder to maintain intimacy and even to find time to be together.

Changes in the sexual relationship frequently begin during pregnancy. One study found that about one fourth of all women reported a decreased desire for sexual intercourse during pregnancy, although this was not necessarily accompanied by a decrease in sexual activity.[11] Men report a wide range of feelings, but most commonly, they have trouble believing that sex will not hurt a woman, particularly after the pregnancy becomes physically obvious. Other men believe their wives are less interested in sex. When the experience of pregnancy is new to both partners, it often leads to less communication about sexual feelings and desires.

Most couples report a decrease in frequency of sexual intercourse as pregnancy progresses. In one study, women reported having sexual relations two to five times a week prior to conception. During the first and second trimesters, sexual activity declined little. By the seventh month, it had declined to 63 percent of previous activity levels; by the eighth month, to less than 50 percent; and it was down to 23 percent of regular activity during the ninth month. No women reported having no sexual intercourse at the beginning of the study, but by about the ninth month, about 60 percent reported having no sexual intercourse.[12]

Usually, though, a couple's sexual life resumes a few weeks after the baby is born, with some adjustments. The best picture of how a couple's sexual relationship changes comes not from statistics but from reports of personal experience. Practically all parents agree that they and their sexual lives suffer from a lack of time, spontaneity, and freedom. One woman, for example, spoke about the dilemma of trying to steal some privacy when there is a two-year-old in the house: "He can get out of the crib by himself. You can imagine what his little face peering into our bedroom has done to our sexual spontaneity on Sunday morning, for example. I was reading something the other day—advice from an expert about whether or not it was healthy for children to see their parents making love. He suggested putting a lock on the bedroom door to keep children out. That really made me laugh. You just don't lock out your child, and you never leave a two-year-old roaming free and unsupervised for even a minute. A lock on the bedroom door. It's a nice thought, but totally unrealistic. Do you know any parents who have a lock on their bedroom door?"

Another woman said, "Sex just becomes less free, more planned, once you have children. When our children were little, we just settled into a bedtime routine whereas before we had often made love in the morning. After the baby, we were too tired to do much of anything for a while. Then, there was a period there when the kids were little when the routine time was Saturday night. Bob commuted during the week and he was too tired, and I was beat from being with the kids all day. Now we have a lot more freedom since the kids are older and go off by themselves fairly often."

Some couples, highly nurturing ones who have always known that children would be part of their marriage, find the trade-off of less sex—or less spontaneous sex—a fair exchange for the rewards of parenthood. In fact, for many, the task of parenting is so enjoyable that it replaces the intense sexual desire for each other, at least during the early, most hectic years of child rearing.

One young mother of two toddlers said, "I never would have believed it if anyone had told me, but I enjoy my sexual relationship just as much with my husband even though it is less passionate now than it was before the kids were born. I don't think we feel less passionately about each other, but we do have less time alone together. Still, it's a period in our lives that will pass, and all too quickly, we feel, so we don't mind. And we do leave the kids with my parents every once in a while so we can have a weekend all to ourselves."

Because these people did not expect to be sexually enthralled with one another in the same way they were before becoming parents, they often speak of replacing this passion with a deeper feeling that offers new satisfactions to both partners; others fear this loss of intensity and spontaneity. The only way a couple can know which type they are is through careful self-analysis and evaluation of their relationship. Each couple must weigh carefully how much a part of their marriage their sexual life is and how willing they are to change the emotional timbre of it. When expression of these fears dominates any conversation about whether or not to have children, that is a sign that a couple may resent any changes in this area of their life. Because it is difficult to predict exactly what the changes will be for any couple, or whether they will be unpleasant ones, it is important to air and probe any feelings before having a child.

The Interpersonal Changes

In a sense, the problems that can crop up with regard to money and sexual relationships are rather cut-and-dried in that they are usually easy to identify, discuss, and even resolve. Most persons have enough perception and self-awareness to be able to predict with a fair amount of accuracy how they will react to living on less money or living with a less spontaneous or less passionate sexual life. Less predictable—and thus more difficult to resolve—are the interpersonal changes that typically occur in a marriage with the birth of a child.

Research has shown that the birth of a child frequently leads to a shift in the structure of the marriage. Most American marriages fit into one of two styles. They are either patriarchal, which means that the husband tends to be dominant, or they are egalitarian, which means that responsibilities are shared. For many years, the patriarchal marriage was the most common pattern in the United States, but under the influence of the women's movement and other changes in social values that have occurred in the past few decades, many more couples have shaped their marriages in the egalitarian mold. Research indicates, though, that marriages that are egalitarian in the early child-free years often shift into a patriarchal mold with the birth of the first child—and therein lies the rub, for most women, at least.

The reason for the shift is all too obvious, and it is usually psychological and physical. The wife retires from work or takes off a protracted amount of time to care for the child; far less often does this burden fall to the husband. Without her paycheck and the sense of independence she frequently associates with it, she becomes more dependent upon her husband. To compensate for not bringing home a paycheck, she often takes on more of the household chores at the very time when she is already engaged in full-time child care. Several studies have shown that when the wife works full time in the home, the husband begins to help less often. Both partners, often for different reasons, assume that since she is home all day, she can handle all the domestic routine. The husband thinks this is simply a matter of logistics. Never having cared for a child, he is unaware how time-consuming it is, and for that matter, never having maintained a household by himself, particularly one that includes an infant, he sees no reason that his wife should not do all the domestic work now that she has "free" time. For the woman, this is a matter of compensation: without the clout her paycheck gave her, she begins to feel she can no longer expect her husband to do half or even any share of the housework. Over time, it becomes apparent that they are no longer equals in their marriage and that the marriage is no longer egalitarian.

In addition to any physical changes in each partner's roles within the marriage, a more subtle realignment of roles is also occurring. Neither partner may want or welcome this shift, as the marriage changes even more from an egalitarian to a patriarchal mode, but

the change still occurs, often so subtly that neither partner under-
stands what is happening. Unfortunately, they occur at a point in
the couple's lives when they have less time together than ever
before to sit down and sort out things. The presence of a child—
even pregnancy and childbirth—is often especially disruptive to an
egalitarian marriage. This is doubly true when both partners have
struggled to carve out a marriage in which they function as equals.

The woman may resent the extra work and new responsibilities.
Since she has worked, often at a career that was important to her,
she may feel resentment over that loss. Many women feel they
have, although perhaps only temporarily, lost their independence—
and even their identities. Her husband, eager to help, may inadver-
tently go about doing so the wrong way. His tack often is to assume a more protective attitude—in fact, to become the family's
sole caretaker. In return for her caring for his child, he would like
to take care of her while she is so occupied as a mother. But she
may resist this, perhaps to the surprise of them both. For the first
time in their marriage, husband and wife may find they are at odds
with each other (and within themselves, for that matter) over their
interpersonal roles and responsibilities.

By contrast, the marriage of a couple who have had a patriarchal
relationship all along may well blossom with the addition of a
baby. By taking on the role of mother, the woman feels more valuable within the marriage. Through fatherhood, the man is able to
expand his patriarchal empire. His protectiveness is, at last, truly
needed. Becoming parents is, for such persons, often a source of
narcissistic satisfaction, especially when compared to an egalitarian
marriage, where adding a baby can spell disaster unless both partners are alerted to the potential for danger.

The changes are usually most burdensome for the woman, particularly if she has worked for many years before becoming a mother.
A woman who has not resolved her ambivalence about children
may find the sudden shift into her new role of parent fraught with
almost unbearable frustration. The contrast between a freewheel-
ing career woman and a mother whose every hour is tied to caring
for an infant who is totally dependent upon her is almost impossible for most women to imagine without having experienced motherhood. Her life changes, with frightening suddenness, the first day
she is left alone with her baby. Aside from the need to cope with

an unfamiliar and totally dependent being, a woman awakens on her first day home alone with her baby to find that, in twenty-four hours or less, she has become an entirely new person. For several years, she has gotten up every morning, dressed, and left the house to pursue her career. If she is like many working women, her career has been a primary source of her self-definition; it helped her find herself in her postcollege years. If she delayed childbearing into her mid- or late thirties, her interest in her career probably only intensified. Now suddenly, all that is gone, at least for a while. The longer a woman has taken to establish herself in a career, the more difficult she may find the transition to motherhood, and the more she may take out her frustration and unhappiness on her husband, whose life has changed far less than hers.

At the very time when a woman also may be counting on moral support and encouragement from her husband, he may be feeling neglected and at a loss over what is expected of him. In *The Quality of American Life,* thirty-two husbands were asked how they reacted to their first child. Sixteen men said they sometimes felt neglected, and four men often felt neglected. Only twelve men said they never felt neglected. In the same study, two thirds of the wives experienced guilt because they felt they neglected their husbands, and twelve of the wives felt their husbands neglected them.[13]

These feelings point to a lack of understanding between spouses brought on, at least in part, by the birth of a child. According to the same study, understanding between spouses was lower among women with young children than any other group of women. And while 65 percent of men with no children or men whose children had grown thought their wives understood them "very well," only 43 percent of men with small children felt their wives understood them. Problems in understanding one another and feelings of neglect may be compounded by the fact that there is far less time in which to communicate with one another after the baby is born since a couple's time together is cut in half by the birth of a baby.[14]

Are Childless Marriages Happier than Those of Parents?

The ultimate question for parents, childless couples, and the experts is whether couples who are childless have happier marriages, as has been reported, than do those who become parents. Childless couples often cite studies showing they are happier than married couples with children, and parents in response wave around the higher divorce rate of childless couples. Parents warn that people who decide not to have children will have regrets later.

One mother of three declared, "They may be taking their pleasure now, but it's selfish pleasure. It's true I'm completely absorbed in my children right now, and I know that's not very chic in these times, but I believe I am making an investment in my future. I will have my children to comfort me when I'm old, when childless women won't have anyone."

Particularly in these days when childlessness has acquired a certain degree of cachet, childless couples have a ready response. A typical reply is this from a forty-four-year-old childless woman, who said, "I think it's selfish to have children so you'll have someone to look after you when you're old. Look at how many children can't stand their parents, how begrudgingly they give time to them. I also think parents are jealous of my life-style. We used to be outcasts because we didn't have any children, but now our lives look pretty good, even glamorous. My husband and I enjoy ourselves. We spend money on things we want rather than emergencies."

Despite the rhetoric on both sides, there is no way to say who is right or wrong. Mostly, the conflicting views just point up the futility of making such blanket comparisons between groups when the personalities and circumstances of individuals' lives are what really determine marital happiness. In fact, comparing the marriages of childless couples to those of parents is a little like comparing apples and oranges. In both cases, the comparison fails because the objects being compared are so completely different despite any seeming similarities. Certainly, both parenting and childlessness have their own special benefits and pleasures, and both have their own drawbacks.

There are, however, some interesting conclusions to be drawn from examining the marriages of childless couples vis-à-vis those of parents. Among married couples with children, researchers have long been aware of a dip in marital satisfaction in the middle years of marriage, mostly when the couple are in their forties. For a long time, no one thought to correlate this dip to the presence of young children in the home. A connection was made, however, and researchers have now concluded that children are a cause of marital dissatisfaction during the middle years of marriage.

One reason so much time was required to make this simple connection was that most researchers did not include childless couples so they had no control groups against which to compare and contrast what they were finding out about parents' marital dissatisfactions. For example, Boyd Rollins and Harold Feldman, leading researchers on this subject, reported that twelve studies showed a decline in marital happiness over the first ten years of marriage, until the children go to school, but none of these studies included childless couples because they were considered "atypical."[15]

Rollins and Feldman surveyed couples before and after they have had children to measure changes in marital satisfaction. All couples report that they experience the most happiness in the period immediately after marriage. With the birth of the first child, there follows a period of disruption in the marriage, which turns into several years of relatively low marital satisfaction while the children are being reared.[16] The children's needs tend to take precedence over any needs of the parents. And parents—especially mothers—become intensely involved in their children. In a survey conducted in the mid-1960s, 38 percent of married women reported motherhood as their primary source of satisfaction while only 8 percent said marriage was, and suburban women favored the role of mother more than urban women did.[17] Another report of 600 suburban women in their thirties found that women viewed their husbands first as breadwinners, second as fathers, and third as husbands.[18]

Most marriages do not enter a period of high satisfaction again until the children leave home. Even then, emotional snags can create disharmony. Many women experience "empty nest" syndrome when their children leave home, particularly if they have been full-time mothers. Many marriages undergo some conflict when the husband retires. At a time when one would expect a marriage to run especially smoothly, new and potentially marriage-threatening conflicts arise.

In contrast, during the rocky period for parents when children are in the home, childless couples report feeling highly in tune with one another's feelings and needs. They communicate well with one another and tend to think of themselves as friends rather than as marriage partners; they do more things together than parents do.[19]

In *The Quality of American Life,* researchers also noted that childless couples did not differ from those with children in their feelings of satisfaction with family life. The researchers concluded that "parenthood is clearly not essential to a sense of family and a satisfaction with that association."[20] The differences were obvious enough to lead the researchers to conclude:

> Despite the fact that these marriages might be regarded as un-fulfilled (married women, 29 and over, no children) in terms of prevailing cultural norms, these women do not describe their lives in more negative terms than people at other stages of the life cycle. While childless wives over 29 are somewhat less positive than younger (under 30) married women with no children in their general sense of well-being, they are more positive than the average of all women.[21]

Assuming these studies are accurate, childless couples may not have happier marriages so much as they have less disruptive relationships. They may even have to work a little harder than parents to inject excitement into their relationships because their marriages are not punctuated with the crises of childbirth and child rearing. Parents, on the other hand, tend to derive fulfillment from their children rather than from their marriages during the period when marital satisfaction dips. They are, therefore, not leading dissatisfied lives so much as they are redirecting the focus of their satisfaction. And furthermore, parents expect to—and often do—reenter a period of deep satisfaction with their marriages after their children leave home.

Critics of childless marriages often point to the fact that divorce is more frequent among childless couples, but this is probably one of the more humane results of the loosening of moral strictures in the last twenty years. People now feel more free to escape the bonds of an unhappy marriage. Research shows that unhappily married couples often stay together only for the children, which has to be its own kind of prison, as relationships go.

Eleanore Luckey and Joyce Bain, in a survey of eighty couples, half of whom had satisfactory marriages and half of whom had unsatisfactory ones, found that children were often the only source of marital satisfaction for unhappily married couples. By contrast, companionship was found to be a more important source of marital satisfaction to couples who were happily married.[22]

In other words, unhappily married couples who stay together for the sake of the children are not necessarily any happier than unhappily married childless couples who find their marriages easier to dissolve because they have no children—childless couples simply feel more free than parents to escape from an unhappy marriage.

The Special Dissatisfactions of Women

The fact that women tend to suffer more in marriage than men was a major thrust of the book *The Future of Marriage* by sociologist Jessie Bernard, who came to believe that marriage was often a pathological state for many women:

> In 1970, Margaret Mead was quoted by Robert Williams as warning women in the Women's Liberation Movement that they might literally be driving men insane. The reverse seems more likely. It is wives who are driven mad, not by men but by the anachronistic way in which marriage is structured today—or rather, the life-style which accompanies marriage today and which demands that all wives be housewives. In truth, being a housewife makes women sick.[23]

An immediate response is that fewer than 50 percent of women are full-time housewives in the 1980s, so this is less of a problem. But the changes in women's lives may only have added to their emotional and physical burdens rather than diminished them. In fact to note that women are no longer housewives is something of a misrepresentation of women's plight today. While many women do enjoy the benefits associated with a career outside the home, most women have managed to achieve these benefits by adding their careers to their more traditional work load as wives and mothers. Their burdens and responsibilities have only increased; thus, there is reason to believe that they may be even more likely to be driven crazy than women a generation ago whose major burdens were motherhood and housewifery. Today, women cope not only with the traditional domestic work load, but also with the work load of an outside job and with the pressures to succeed in a male-dominated world.

Some researchers have found that disenchantment with marriage sets in for a woman only when she has children. Rollins and Feldman wrote:

> For the wives there was a definite pattern. There was a sharp increase in the frequency of negative feelings with the arrival of the first child and then a leveling off until the "teenage" stage where a substantial decline in negative feelings began and continued to the "launching" stage, leveling out through the "retirement" stage.[24]

Childless women also tend to feel that marriage is less restrictive than do mothers. Forty-eight percent of mothers feel marriage is restrictive, for example, while 35 percent of childless women do. Childless women fall into the same category as men, regardless of whether the men are fathers; 39 percent of fathers feel marriage is restrictive and 34 percent of childless men feel it is. In addition, 54 percent of mothers report problems with their marriages, while only 31 percent of fathers do. Among childless couples, 39 percent of women and 31 percent of men reported marital problems. Forty-six percent of mothers rate themselves as "very happy" compared with 51 percent of childless women, 49 percent of fathers, and 60 percent of childless men. Somewhat surprisingly, given the cultural pressure on women to become mothers, childless women did not report significantly higher feelings of inadequacy (9 percent) than did mothers (8 percent) or self-dissatisfaction (6 percent for mothers, 4 percent for childless women). Most surprising of all was the difference in self-dissatisfaction between fathers (16 percent) and childless men (8 percent).[25]*

Recognizing that childlessness may contribute to a happier mar-

---

* These figures, the most recent available, were compiled in 1970. Given the direction of social change, particularly the lessening of pressure on women to have children, one might expect the gaps to be even larger today, in the 1980s, in the categories of women's sense of marriage's restrictiveness, marital problems, happiness, and self-dissatisfaction. They may even have changed to the point where mothers, who are more likely to work as full-time housewives, may have greater feelings of inadequacy than working, childless women. One is also tempted to speculate that fewer fathers would be experiencing self-dissatisfaction, given the social encouragement they now receive to express their nurturing feelings.

riage and resolving the ambivalence so many couples experience over whether or not to have children, however, are two different matters entirely. Furthermore, how much of a crisis a baby will precipitate in any one marriage depends on so many personal factors that there is often no way to make predictions for individual couples. But one thing is certain: where one or both marriage partners are ambivalent about children, a child *is* more likely to precipitate a marital crisis than when both persons eagerly want a child. If the ambivalence is not resolved, in almost all cases, a child will only magnify it; it will not cause it to disappear magically, as so many people hope. Too many childless couples avoid airing their feelings about children and the effect a child will have on their marriage before they have a child.

Marie Burnett, a psychologist who has worked with many persons experiencing parental ambivalence, notes that rarely are both partners equally ambivalent. She thinks this may contribute to the feeling that a couple is going round and round over the issue or that the issue of ambivalence is basically unresolvable. She commented, "The ambivalence, in fact, usually expresses itself by one person wanting a child and the other person not wanting a child. They both may be ambivalent, but they tend to take opposite stands when they discuss their feelings. Often, one partner resolves the ambivalence, and the other person becomes dubious again. That can go on and on."[26]

According to Burnett, the ambivalence can be resolved only when the root issues are uncovered and examined, and for some couples, therapy is helpful in this process. She commented, "There are different sets of issues. Ambivalence over children can be unresolvable until the couple teases out the top layer and finds out what the real problems are. There may be problems about the mechanics of rearing a child—who will stay home, who will do most of the work. Will the wife have to give up her career? Will the husband make a real investment in rearing a child? When a couple gets to this level, the ambivalence is often resolvable, especially if each person is willing to compromise. If she only wants a commitment that he will be a coparent, and he is willing to give that commitment, then this couple may well resolve their ambivalence and become parents."[27]

Other issues that appear to involve only one partner are nonetheless problems for the couple, and some of these, Burnett and other therapists agree, may necessitate long-term therapy. This might be the case in a relationship where one partner experienced a childhood that had created a deep-seated fear of becoming the parent that he or she resented or hated.

For example, for some years, a rather dismal prognosis has been usual for women (and men, for that matter) who were abused children. The prevalent feeling among therapists was that these people are more likely than others to be child abusers themselves because, among other factors, of the patterns of parenting they observed as they were growing up. Burnett, who takes a more optimistic view of the man or woman who was a battered child and who is reluctant to become a parent because of this, noted, "The notion that abused children become abusing parents is true if that abused child never acquires any insight into what has happened to her. But once this person receives some intervention, once she achieves a strong nurturing relationship with a therapist, then, of course, she can become a nurturing parent. Some of these people will need support all during the time their children are growing up. But it is not inevitable that an abused child will always become an abusing parent. That is a kind of ambivalence that can be resolved."[28]

Ironically, another kind of ambivalence that requires long-term therapy is one that rarely surfaces without therapy but which is nonetheless a serious problem for many seemingly traditional women. Burnett explained, "These women believe if you are total female, then you want a child. If you don't want a child, then you're not feminine. This woman may not be able to verbalize her ambivalence, and instead, she may develop a physical symptom that is actually psychological: she may become sterile, for example, although for no apparent reason. This woman also must get in touch with her ambivalence and accept that it is all right to feel it. Her conflicts are largely unconscious, and the therapist who works with this kind of woman needs to do a lot of consciousness raising so the woman can really accept that she may not want children and that this is an acceptable choice for her."[29]

When a woman is working out such serious issues, the support of her husband is vital, and of course, he may need some help in adjusting to her new understanding of herself.

Another kind of ambivalence that affects couples and that may best be resolved in a therapist's office, unless the individuals are very perceptive, is ambivalence that is obsessive. When a couple cannot leave the subject of children alone for any length of time, according to Burnett, when they cannot stop thinking about how they would feel if a child they had were seriously ill or handicapped, they may be candidates for childlessness.

Burnett added, "To have the courage to have a baby, one has to allow for at least 25 percent blindness. One doesn't know whether one will have a healthy child, one without handicaps. There are so many unknowns. People who need 100 percent control usually panic when they find out they are going to be parents. These people might have been better off having no children. If you need a lot of control, you aren't going to be a very healthy parent, and you are not going to have healthy children."[30]

Many kinds of problems that arise with ambivalent couples can be resolved with therapy, and many couples will learn, in the course of therapy, that they do want children, after all. Many signs, however, point to the fact that for some couples childlessness is the right answer, despite society's continued pressure on married couples to reproduce. Bernard was among the first to connect marital happiness and childlessness and to write about it cogently, and the ranks of experts who agree with her are swelling. She is optimistic about the future of childless marriages:

If it weren't for babies and children, the problems associated with marriage, though never easy, would be vastly simplified. Men and women would continue to love each other and cease to love each other; they would continue to attract and cease to attract each other—but in ways quite different from those that characterize relationships in which children are involved. Already there is unofficial recognition of marriages with and without children. If there are no children, divorce is easier to get. And if, in addition, there is little property involved, marriage does, indeed, become a very private affair. To the extent that childlessness becomes common in the future, marriage will be increasingly private and personal, and, for many husbands and wives, also more satisfactory.[31]

4.
THE HIGH COST OF BRINGING UP BABY

For years, society's message to young married couples has been: "Have children now and worry later about how to pay for them." Sociologist Judith Blake put her finger on society's attitude toward the cost of a family when she wrote that the expenditures entailed by having a baby for a couple who cannot afford one are "regarded quite differently from their decision to purchase a consumer durable they cannot afford."[1] Indeed, if you buy a house or a car that is beyond your means, you will likely encounter some societal disapproval. Despite the fact that Americans are an increasingly credit-oriented society, financial responsibility is considered a social obligation, particularly for families.

Until very recently, when the phenomenon of two-career couples gave many young people unprecedented earning power, an escalating standard of living was regarded—and applauded—as accepted social behavior expected of young couples. A couple, often newly married, might buy a house or car that neither would have purchased as single people, but there was also the expectation that they would buy within their means. If they could not afford a large house, they would buy a smaller one and live in it until they had become sufficiently affluent to move on to a larger one. If they could not afford a house at all, they would live in rented quarters and save their money until they could.

But until recently, when the "purchase" (consumer durable) was a baby, society's expectations for the couple changed. Somehow, a baby was exempt from the notion that a couple should buy only what they could afford. To an extent, there was some feeling that a couple should get on their feet financially before becoming parents, but for the most part, couples were encouraged to have children whether or not they could afford them. Financial disaster seemed to lie ahead for the young couple who spent $180,000 on their first house, but the realization that the same amount of money would be required to rear one child to age eighteen never seemed to cross anyone's mind. Even the idea of evaluating whether or not a baby was affordable was slightly abhorrent to most people. Rather than being considered a "consumer durable" in the same way that a house or car was, a baby took on the magical aura of an inalienable right. But there was a catch: a baby was expensive, something that too many parents learned only after the fact.

Today, however, despite a small undercurrent of guilt, many young couples are weighing the financial costs of having a child prior to making their final decision to be parents. Ironically, these couples are not only those waging an uphill battle against the economy just to stay in the middle class but also the newly affluent two-career couples who are trying to figure out whether they can afford to have a child.

All this is further complicated by the changes in women's lives over the past two decades. When more and more middle-class women went to work outside the home (poor women, of course, have always worked outside the home) in the 1960s, it was mostly to enable their families to buy luxuries that they could no longer afford on the man's salary. Today, however, many of these same women work to buy necessities or simply to maintain a middle-class standard of living.

For women who have only recently graduated and begun to work, the picture is somewhat rosier. While women's incomes still lag behind those of men, young women today are being presented with professional opportunities and accompanying large salaries that make their incomes as important as the man's in maintaining a couple's standard of living. The woman's income in fact often raises their standard of living considerably above what it would be if only the man worked. This is the situation with many professional, two-career couples—the very ones who theoretically can most afford children but who, ironically, make up the group that is most ambivalent about having them.

For both ambivalent and nonambivalent couples, though, the issue of whether or not they can afford a child is riddled with many questions. Will or should the woman give up her career if she has a child? Can a couple subsist, even for a few years, on one income? What professional sacrifices, often referred to as "lost-opportunity costs," will a woman make if she drops out of the work force even temporarily? And particularly for two-career families, is the couple willing to make what may amount to a drastic reduction in their standard of living?

For no other reason than because they are today almost a new social class, perhaps the most interesting couples are those whom John Kenneth Galbraith in his book *The Affluent Society* dubbed the "New Elite." They are well educated, professional, two-income —and affluent.

Childlessness and the New Elite

The rise of the New Elite can be traced to the increase in the number of college degrees—38 percent in 1978 compared to 15 percent in 1948; the growth of jobs in technical and professional areas —from 7.5 percent of all jobs in 1940 to 15.7 percent in 1978; and the increased mobility of Americans and a change in the ways of viewing traditional family life. This new professional class has been deemed significant enough to be the subject of a 1980 symposium at which Harvard scholar Daniel Bell, an authority on changing class structures, commented that the New Elite represent a "mentality, not a class."[2] Those who comprise the New Elite are often described as somewhat detached emotionally, materialistic, and conservative, with a cautious, controlled idealism.

There is one salient feature of these couples' lives that is not so often touched on, and that is their ambivalence about whether or not to have children, which is gradually turning into permanent childlessness for many of them. These are people who could, at least on paper, afford to have as many children as they wanted. Many of them, however, are unable to decide to have even one.

For example, consider Anita and Ed Webster, both thirty-five years old and residents of a posh high-rise condominium on

Chicago's Near North Side.* They are a couple married ten years who are trying to decide whether or not to have a baby. Actually, they are trying to decide whether or not they can afford a baby. The Websters are not poor by anyone's standards—together, they earn more than $50,000 a year. The Websters are typical members of the New Elite: a young, two-income, professional couple who can afford anything they want. Well, almost anything. The Websters think they may not be able to afford a baby. And they are not alone. Partly, the Websters and other young couples like them have gotten used to their affluence, and they are not sure they are willing to lower their standard of living, which they would surely have to do for at least a few years if they have a child. But their story is not simply that of two people who are unwilling to make the sacrifices required to have children. There are more complicated issues at stake, which emerge from conversations with the Websters, issues related to changing social mores and expectations.

Anita Webster tells her story: "I started work in 1968 as a secretary. I think I earned $5,600 on my first job. I thought I would work a couple of years and then get married and have a family. Although I did not enjoy secretarial work and felt that I was entitled to something more after four years of college, I didn't know what I wanted. I took the job mostly because the benefits were so good. It's hard to believe this now, but a four-week vacation after five years sounded great to someone who had loafed every summer of her life.

"But the women's movement came along, and suddenly my firm was looking for women to promote. There I was—ready and waiting. I got a job in the supplies department. My company makes computers and I started out taking phone orders for supplies from our various plants. That didn't excite me, but working with people did. After some thought, and after talking to my boss, I decided that I wanted to go into sales training. Now I assist the vice president of sales training. I write or supervise the writing of our sales training programs, design and order everything salespeople need to

* Both the couples used as case studies in this chapter are real, although pseudonyms have been used here as elsewhere and certain aspects of their lives have been changed to ensure their privacy. I have chosen to include surnames for the first time to simplify references to them.

work efficiently. It feels creative to me, and I like having a job where I am responsible for several things instead of just one. I also train people, and I go out on the road to talk with customers to determine what they need in sales and service. And now I earn $23,000 a year, which sometimes looks like a lot of money to me and at other times looks like an amazingly small amount. It looks small when we're paying our bills."

After obtaining an M.B.A., Ed Webster went to work for a large bank at a salary of $15,000 a year. Last year, after five years there, he changed jobs, which boosted his salary to $30,000 a year. The Websters' combined income is $53,000, and their disposable, after-tax income is around $37,000. They own their apartment, which costs them $1,100 a month, or $13,200 a year, about one third of their combined incomes, in mortgage and maintenance. Their apartment has three bedrooms and could easily accommodate a child.

Actually, Ed and Anita Webster seem like prime candidates to become parents. They have a stable marriage; they have both worked long enough to have built up a healthy savings account, and they earn enough money. Or do they? What may stop the Websters from becoming parents is their financial situation. Anita explains: "Frankly, we both wonder if we would be able to live on what Ed makes—without having to really change our life-style, which would make us unhappy. After all, we've gotten used to living the way we do."

Without Anita's paycheck, the Websters' income would drop to $30,000, or about $22,000 after taxes. After making mortgage and maintenance payments, they would have only $8,800 to cover their remaining living expenses—food, car and other transportation, clothes, medical—as well as the costs of rearing a child. Like many people, Anita and Ed are not particularly realistic about what a baby costs, so they are surprised to learn that having a child would require, in their case, approximately 20 percent of their annual disposable income, or about $4,200.

Anita also acknowledges that she is far more involved with her career than she ever expected to be: "I always thought work was something to fill in the time until I had a baby. I majored in liberal arts in college, and even after I graduated, I had no serious career plans. Now, however, I've got a career. I've gotten some success, and I'm earning more money than I ever thought I would earn. I think I'm hooked, to my surprise."

The Websters enjoy frequent evenings out consisting of dinner at moderately expensive restaurants, followed by theater. Both have cultivated two pricey but presently affordable pastimes in skiing and photography. Their luxuries would take a different form if they decided to have a child. Rather than buying expensive photography equipment and skiing in Europe every year, the Websters would be more likely to take a domestic vacation every two or three years; buy airline tickets to visit grandparents who live at the opposite end of the country; buy a second car, which will have become a necessity where it once may have been a luxury; and save money to send their child to summer camp, pay for orthodontic treatment, and pay for a college education.

The Websters are fortunate in having been able to earn a living that would have boggled the minds of their grandparents and parents at a similar age, but there is a catch. They have done so only by combining their two fairly substantial incomes into one that greatly raises their standard of living. Their plan to live on Ed's income while Anita rears a child is probably not realistic, as they are beginning to see for themselves.

Ed's and Anita's problems may not seem important to some people. After all, they would still be comfortably ensconced in the middle class even if they had a child, and they have had several years of relatively high living. In one sense, perhaps they should be ready to make the necessary sacrifices in order to start a family. Perhaps they are being selfish. But when asked about the way that their standard of living would change, each expressed fears that are real to them and that can easily strike an emotional chord in any one of us.

Ed said, "That's really something, isn't it? Here we are feeling well off, like we can do anything we want to do, go anywhere we want to go. Obviously, we expect to give up some things if we have a child, and we know kids aren't cheap to raise, but it looks as if we'll be moving from the upper class to the lower middle class. I'm not sure I want to spend my life struggling—especially after never having had to struggle at all. Earning good money has always been easy for us so far. My parents, who had their kids right away after they married, struggled for years to get where we are."

Anita said, "I really enjoy our life the way it is. I love my husband and share many interests with him. All that would change if I had a child, and on top of that change, our economic picture would also change. That's a pretty big sacrifice, and frankly, I'm not sure I want to make it. I don't know, maybe we've waited too long and gotten too much to give it all up."

Ed and Anita are expressing a kind of ambivalence that is typical of many other couples in their situation. They have careers they enjoy; they lead interesting lives; and both are very aware of how all this might change were they to become parents. Not too poor to have children, they would still have to make major adjustments in their lives if they choose to have children.

Ed and Anita are likely candidates to join the growing ranks of couples in their late twenties and thirties who are now drifting into childlessness. As one woman said of herself and her husband, they will "wake up one morning and say to themselves, 'Isn't it nice that we never had children?'" thereby acknowledging what time has made a *fait accompli*.

But there is another possible scenario for the Websters, who are already nervously voicing guilt over their ambivalence toward children by repeating to anyone who will listen: "I suppose we're the very ones—educated, well off—who should be having children." By not expressing their fears and discussing them with one another, by assuming a rather blasé attitude overall, they leave themselves open for still deeper guilt feelings and recriminations later on.

If their ambivalence is based on their financial status and professional achievement, two issues that are almost always intertwined in ambivalent couples, then they should confront their feelings more openly, perhaps by asking themselves how their lives will change financially and professionally if they have children. As with other issues that bother couples who are unable to decide whether to have children, their solution may have to be open-ended. The Websters could evaluate their lives and decide they want no children now, but leave the door open for more discussion later. For reasons that will be discussed later in this book, this is not always the very best solution, but it is better than ignoring the ambivalence and letting the guilt grow. Couples who belong to the New Elite are especially susceptible to this.

*

Also candidates for childlessness, although not for the same reasons as the Websters, are the Porters. John Porter, age twenty-seven, and Katie, age twenty-nine, live in Columbus, Indiana. John works as a programmer for the city's major manufacturer, where he earns an annual salary of $18,000. Katie works as a bookkeeper for a small accounting firm, and she earns $9,500 annually. Together, they earn $27,500, and their take-home income is about $23,000.

The Porters always thought their lives would follow a pattern similar to that of their parents and, for that matter, their grandparents. Both have close ties to their families, and they cherish those relationships. They have chosen to live near their families, even though they both would earn more money if they moved to a nearby city such as Indianapolis or Chicago. Unlike the Websters, who never discussed children before marriage, the Porters have talked about how many children they would like. The Porters used to know they wanted four children. Now, ten years after their marriage, they are no longer sure they want any.

Katie and John Porter had always assumed she would stay home to rear children, which would mean a reduction in their after-tax income to about $15,300. They knew they could not live on this amount comfortably, especially if they were also paying for a child. The alternative would have been for Katie to continue to work and to hire someone to care for their child. The possibilities ranged from a full-time, live-in housekeeper or nanny, which would have cost a minimum of $10,000 a year, to day care, which would have cost $800 to $4,000, depending upon whether it was privately or publicly supported, to finding a woman who would have cared for their child in her home, possibly along with several other babies, for a minimum of $60 to $100 a week. The Porters could not have afforded full-time help or, for that matter, private day care, but there are no acceptable public day-care facilities in their community, a not unusual situation outside major urban areas. They would most likely have ended up paying a woman who cared for other people's small children in her home to care for their child while they worked. Sometimes this results in excellent day care; more often, such caretakers are harried housewives and mothers trying to earn extra money for their own families. Furthermore, these mothers are often unlicensed as child caretakers and unskilled in caring for groups of children. Even this kind of care, however, would have cost a third to more than half of Katie's take-home pay.

Katie and John also worry about where they would live. They have been saving for years to buy a house. But ever since they have had enough money for a down payment, interest rates and home prices have been too high for them to handle. They now live in a one-bedroom apartment; if they were to have a child, some kind of new arrangements for housing would become necessary.

Said Katie: "I guess the biggest reason we are not having a baby is money. We just don't see how we can afford a child. Or at least, that is what we started out telling ourselves. But now I think we are becoming ambivalent for other reasons, too—like maybe we've gotten older, and not having children just gets easier as you get older. But mostly, we just can't afford one. If our financial situation were to change, I think we would be much more inclined to have a family."

The Porters are typical of many middle-income couples who, twenty years ago, would have started a family at this point in their marriages and worried later about how to pay for it. Today, though, for people like the Porters, to have a child would entail an even more drastic change in their lives than for the Websters. And since Katie could not afford to stay home full time, having children would be made even more difficult by the problem of finding affordable, reliable child care.

For the Porters, far more than for the Websters, ambivalence about children stems in large part from fears that they cannot afford a child. Although this possibility may not be pleasant to contemplate, it is one of the easier issues for them to deal with, and it is best dealt with before other issues crop up to add to the confusion.

In a sense, the Porters have almost postponed their decision too long. While it was clear to them for several years that money was the primary reason they were not having children, and while it is still the major reason, they are now wondering if they have not grown too old to want to cope with children. This may be a perfectly realistic fear, or it may be a rationalization that makes the whole idea of childlessness more palatable to them. Either way, the Porters are not confronting the issues before them. It is especially important that a couple such as the Porters, who for so long believed they would have children, resolve their ambivalence in time to become parents if that is what they choose.

How Much Does a Child Cost?

One thing that would help the Websters and the Porters resolve their ambivalence is to investigate exactly how much they should expect to spend on a child. Any discussion of the cost of children typically produces a naïve shrug from nonparents and a knowing look from parents. Although the idea of placing a monetary value on a child seems cold and harsh, especially in a culture that views children as priceless possessions, ambivalent couples would still do better to face up to the expenses before they leap into parenthood, rather than wake up one morning to find that they have gone from being ambivalent nonparents to ambivalent parents, a situation that has its own costs.

There are many ways to measure the costs of having a child. Apart from the financial costs, there are the emotional costs—the love and psychic energy spent on a child throughout its and its parents' lifetimes. Social scientists use the term "lost-opportunity costs" to describe the time and energy spent at PTA meetings, basketball games, and other events by parents who might prefer, or need, to be elsewhere, as well as the career costs to a person who stays home to rear a child. Most often, it is the woman who makes these sacrifices.

The most measurable costs, however, are economic, yet these, too, are difficult to calculate because there are so many personal variables. For example, two families with the same income are not necessarily in the same overall financial situation, nor do they have the same spending habits. Also impossible to predict is how a family's income will grow during the child-rearing years, except to say that it will probably become larger. Finally, the vagaries of the economy, which have played havoc with many people's lives for the past twenty years, are equally impossible to predict.

Three major changes in economic status are typically associated with the birth of the first child. First, many couples find they need to buy a house or change their living arrangements in some usually more expensive way to accommodate a child. Second, often they must buy a car if they do not own one, or a second car if they do. And third, the woman typically leaves the work force for a period that ranges from several months to several years, thus reducing the family income. These are considered the direct costs of having a child.

A more intangible cost involves the material things that a couple will have to give up if their income drops even temporarily. Couples report that the sacrifices often take the form of fewer or no vacations and no luxuries such as expensive evenings on the town, expensive clothes, furs, or jewelry. (Although it would be interesting to calculate the sum that a couple would have to be compensated to maintain their childless standard of living, only one British social scientist has attempted to do this. Unfortunately, the figures apply only to Great Britain, and they are too outdated to be of any use here.)

Calculating the costs of a child always contains an additional element of unpredictability that results from the fact that no one can know in advance what, if any, special expenses will have to be met because a child is handicapped, chronically ill, or emotionally disturbed. An ill or handicapped child can also mean that the mother will not be able to return to work at all.

Finally, how much of your income will be consumed by a child depends on how much you earn. Poor and middle-class persons spend fewer dollars on their children than do the rich, but those dollars represent a greater chunk of their incomes. One expert estimated that rearing a child in a middle- or low-income family to age eighteen consumes two and a half times the average annual wage of the wage earners.[3]

The richer one is, as noted above, the more one spends on a child, for social pressure demands that the parents' standard of living also apply to the child. Rich kids tend to end up with the usual accoutrements of wealth—lessons in everything from ballet to woodblock printing, summer camp, fancy clothes, expensive entertainment, and lots of toys. If a child attends a private school, the annual costs of elementary and high school are comparable to those of a private college, only these costs are repeated over twelve years rather than four.

Social pressure to produce what might be called "quality children"—to care for them well, educate them well—will, predicts Judith Blake, become even more important in the 1980s as American society becomes increasingly materialistic and people must battle to stay even with a fluctuating economy. She also notes that the parents of only children are highly motivated to have more. Although only children have become more acceptable in recent years, there is still considerable pressure to give an only child siblings—if only as a means of socializing the children.[4]

There also appears to be one special hidden cost. It occurs only when a child is conceived out of wedlock by parents who feel they must marry before the child is born—a common enough occurrence among couples today who live together and who postpone marriage until pregnancy forces a decision. In one study, it was found that a premarital conception can result in a lifelong economic handicap. The most obvious reason was that an unplanned-for marriage often cut off, temporarily or permanently, educational opportunities, but even when adjustments were made for educational levels, people who had to marry because the woman was pregnant still suffered an economic handicap that did not affect other couples who married young or who interrupted their educations to marry. R. H. Reed and Susan McIntosh, the authors of the study, suggested that the handicap resulted from a psychological side effect of going into marriage and parenthood ambivalently.[5] As more and more couples approach parenting without resolving their ambivalence toward it, there is the possibility that this handicap will affect these people too, even if they are married before the baby is conceived.

In 1978 the Health Insurance Institute rather conservatively put the cost of having a baby at about $2,600. This included $700 for a layette, $300 in maternity clothes for the mother, $400 for the obstetrician, and a four-day hospital stay at $145 a day. Miscellaneous costs that made up the remainder included delivery room preparations, nursery fees, laboratory and pathology fees, drugs, hospital supplies, and some of the common extra expenses such as a fetal monitor or, if required, Rh injections for the mother. The Health Insurance Institute found that the *average* hospital room in 1978, however, hovered at around $200 a day, and that a cesarean section, which now is used in about 40 percent of all deliveries, can double the obstetrician's fees.[6]

Since these figures were national averages, the following rundown of one couple's expenses for prenatal and delivery care in Indianapolis, Indiana, for a baby born in 1982 may be more useful:[7]

Obstetrician	$500.00
Hospital room (semiprivate) for mother (4 days)	820.00
Hospital nursery fees	540.00
Pediatrician	40.00
Labor room	288.00
Drugs for baby and mother	107.00
Supplies	162.00
Maternity clothes	200.00
Baby clothes	230.00
Baby furniture (dresser, bed, playpen)	580.00
Total cost	$3,467.00

This mother had a cesarean section, so she incurred the following extra expenses as a result of the surgery:

Physician's fee	$400.00
Anesthesiologist's fee	180.00
Anesthesia	150.00
Laboratory tests	99.00

Including the cesarean, this baby, born in an average, middle-sized American city, cost $4,296.

In large American cities the cost of having a baby in 1980 was estimated at $2,250 to $5,000. A New York *Times* article noted that the obstetrician's bill averages $1,200 to $1,500, with some approaching $2,000. The bill covers regular and frequent office visits, usually ten to fifteen for a normal pregnancy, and also such tests as amniocentesis, which is recommended for older pregnant women to rule out the possibility of several serious disorders. The average hospital stay for childbirth in Manhattan costs $1,500 to $3,000. A cesarean delivery can easily push the hospital costs to $5,000.[8]

Insurance covers some of these costs, but the most generous policies rarely cover more than 80 percent of the obstetrician's fees. Dr. Mordecai A. Berkun, medical director of Blue Cross-Blue

Shield in New York, noted that the typical coverage on a private policy for obstetrician's fees is about $300, although more expensive policies cover up to $725 in obstetrician's fees. Usually, the mother's hospital stay is covered in full by company insurance policies.[9]

Once the first-year crunch is past, experts estimate a child will consume 15–17 percent of a family's annual income.

If the child is sent to college, another major expense will be incurred—and one that is skyrocketing. In 1981 the New York *Times* heralded the arrival of a $10,000-a-year tuition at many private colleges.[10] The cost of tuition in many small or not particularly elite schools hovers between $5,000 to $6,000 a year, and those figures do not take room and board, spending money, or transportation costs into account. In 1982, tuition increases averaged 15 percent, slightly ahead of inflation that year. But educators warned that they had held the line on college costs for many years and that the cost of a college education would probably continue to rise in the coming decade even if inflation abated. Tuition for a run-of-the-mill college education even at a public school in the year 2000 could easily total $40,000.

Special Costs to Women

In addition to the financial cost incurred in physically rearing a child, sociologists have tried to calculate the hidden economic costs, the lost-opportunity costs mentioned earlier. They mostly apply to women, since the wife is more likely to drop her career to care for the child than the husband is. Lost-opportunity costs include the years spent by the woman outside the work force and the subsequent damage to her career, the toll childbearing takes on her health, the added stress and frustration that typically accompanies any traumatic interruption in one's life, the empty-nest syndrome when children leave home, and the frustration experienced when one is not able even for a short period to do the work that one has trained for and desires to do. These are highly intangible things and not easy to measure; a woman can only calculate them by examining her personal feelings and situation carefully.

Lost-opportunity costs seem vague unless you are a woman experiencing them. Then they are very real, if somewhat difficult to

CHILDLESS BY CHOICE

translate into dollars and cents. For example, how does a woman measure the number of promotions she might have received had she not taken time off for motherhood? If she lags behind her male colleagues, how much of this, personal ability aside, can be attributed to being a woman and how much to being a mother? How can a woman measure the frustration of leaving work she loves for another kind of work she may also love but which clearly does not require the high-level skills she used in her career and which is rewarding but also boring and mundane at the same time?

One lost-opportunity cost that has been calculated in dollars is the money a woman loses when she leaves the work force. In 1969, the only time such figures were compiled, a woman with an elementary school education who stayed home for fourteen years to rear children could expect to lose $29,000 in wages; a woman with a high school education, about $40,000; and a woman with a college education, about $55,000.[11] A woman who had done graduate work lost almost $70,000. And these statistics were calculated for 1969, just before women began to make real strides toward economic equality. Today these dollar amounts would be more than double.

About ten years ago Swedish economist Per Holmberg estimated that if women were as well and as fully employed as men, the standard of living would go up by one third.[12] Reed and McIntosh also estimated that a highly educated woman's lost-opportunity costs were approximately three times the direct costs of rearing the child.[13] This means that if a child cost a middle-class family $80,000 to rear from infancy to age eighteen, as the most recent government figures indicate, the mother's lost-opportunity costs will be approximately $240,000.

Today, and this will increasingly be true in the future, women cannot afford to stop working, anyway. In *The Two-Paycheck Marriage*, Caroline Bird wrote that "by 1976, only 40 percent of the jobs in the country paid enough to support a family." Women's incomes, although still far less than men's, quite simply are no longer gravy for most families; they are used to buy the necessities.[14]

The fact that mothers will remain in the work force, however, creates some new and as yet unmeasured lost-opportunity costs that anyone who is contemplating motherhood may want to consider. Mothers who work will lose precious leisure time as they shoulder what amounts to two full-time jobs—their job at home and their job outside the home. They will sacrifice many opportunities that full-time mothers presently enjoy, such as attending school functions in the afternoon; spending large, uninterrupted chunks of time with their children; and possibly even to some degree having the opportunity to be the single major force in shaping their children's lives. Professional mothers often comment that they have had to adjust their egos to just this fact. (Despite all this, there is ample evidence that working women are effective mothers. The time they spend with their children is often highly focused, high-quality time. A working mother's values will continue to dominate her child's life simply because she is the parent.)

Official Policy: "Everyone Can Afford a Baby"

People like the Websters and the Porters present a dilemma. Furthermore, their situations are not so unrelated as they may seem at first glance. Both couples are ambivalent, but if all things were equal, the Websters probably would opt for a child-free life while the Porters would probably have a child. Something needs to be done to ease the plight of both couples, and something can, in fact, be done. Both couples would be the beneficiaries of any reevaluation of the present societal values assigned to children and childlessness.

The belief that everyone can afford babies permeated the 1950s and 1960s. Women often joyfully had three or four children with little or no thought of the cost. Their husbands earned the money to pay for the babies, and everyone encouraged young couples to buy the "product" with no concern for whether or not they could pay for it, as this comment from one physician, made in 1955, indicates:

> Once doubtful feelings are voiced, reassurance can be given by pointing out (1) that unhappiness during the first months of pregnancy is a usual occurrence, and (2) that most women find themselves eager for the baby before it actually arrives despite their earlier feelings. Even financial worries tend to disappear after the birth of the baby *even if there is no money* [italics added].[15]

The sad truth is that American society has been geared toward encouraging everyone—except the mentally deficient—to think they can afford children even when this is not actually the case. And although women have been enjoying the relative freedom of an antinatalist era in the past decade, over the long haul, the United States has mostly been a pronatalist society. It has certainly, for most of its existence, been a culture that does not look with favor on women who choose to remain childless when they might have children. Judith Blake, in her provocative article "Are Babies Consumer Durables?" summed up society's pronatalist view when she wrote:

> Not only are individuals under strong institutional pressure to marry and start a family, but the decision to do so, even in the face of financial difficulties, receives widespread moral (and, if necessary, tangible) encouragement. . . . In sum, although the demand for consumer durables is pegged to purchasing power, the "demand" for children is not under such monetary control. In fact, by creating public support for the dominance of family "values" over economic rationality, reproductive and social institutions are geared to *prevent* economic factors from inhibiting reproduction.[16]

Economic pronatalist incentives are everywhere—they are even built into the tax structure. They include medical and child-care deductions, tax exemptions for children, and tax breaks for homeowners, who are often parents. By contrast, renters, who are statistically less likely to be parents than homeowners, receive no tax breaks. In fact, childless couples do not receive any incentives to remain childless in the present tax structure. Without spending a considerable amount of time and money on investments or owning property, the average childless couple often cannot even itemize their deductions.

Ironically, American society need not be in the business of encouraging babies at all. It could neither encourage nor discourage them, thus taking one more step toward making the issue of whether or not to have children truly one of free choice. Two experts on government policy regarding population growth, Elliott R. Morss and Susan McIntosh Ralph, pointed out that society's pronatalist bias could be changed to a more neutral stance if the government adopted two major policy changes. The first would involve increasing the desirability of alternatives to children, and the second would involve encouraging childlessness and promoting greater control over family size. To this end, Morss and Ralph suggested that the government give tax deductions for activities pursued most often by the childless, such as adult education and travel, in order to balance those given to parents. The government could also, they suggested, become more involved in the dispensing of contraceptives, although this has its dangers,† because the contraceptives could also be withheld from women as a means of promoting childbearing.[17]

The new freedom to remain childless—viewed by some as a welcome loosening of social strictures and by others as a disaster for American family life—has been precipitated as much by economic factors as by social change. And eventually, everyone will lose if this change is not accepted and put into perspective. The Porters will probably not be happy if they remain childless because they believe they cannot afford a child. The Websters could face a serious dilemma if a backlash against childlessness occurs while they are still young enough to have children; they might be pressured into having a child they do not really want to avoid a loss of social esteem.

With the present situation, however, the child-free option is more likely to become attractive even to those who, under other circumstances, might have preferred to have children. If this happens, society will pay the price, since even when a high birth rate is not desirable, some children still are needed to replenish society's natural losses and to satisfy the longings of some people. Furthermore, we now have enough psychological sophistication to realize that people do best what they freely choose to do. Nonetheless, childless couples are increasingly seduced by certain economic advantages that are out of reach to those who become parents.

It may, therefore, be in society's best interests to rethink its pronatalist bias and possibly to attempt to erase all bias. Some tax incentives could be offered to parents, and some could be offered to those who opt for a child-free life. In any case, all persons could

† Witness the recent attempts by government policy makers to deny contraceptives to teenagers.

be encouraged to consider before they had children whether or not they truly wanted to become parents, as well as whether they were willing to make the sacrifices, financial and otherwise, that are necessary if they do become parents.

5.
CAREERS, CREATIVITY, AND CHILDREN

When asked why they are not having babies, most young women who have joined the ranks of the childless, either temporarily or permanently, cite their careers as the major cause of their maternal ambivalence.

One thirty-nine-year-old stockbroker said, "I've enjoyed my career and gotten far more involved than I ever imagined I would when I started out, perhaps because my success was not something I expected. When I started working fifteen years ago, women could not hope for much, either in terms of money or in terms of achievement. So the fact that I've gotten where I am—and that I've had to work very hard to get this far—makes me that much more reluctant to give it all up and have a baby. Work is so much more rewarding than I ever thought it would be."

Another woman, who at age forty-four stands at the pinnacle of success in her chosen field of advertising, commented, "I really always thought I would drop my career and have a baby or babies—I used to think about three or four—the first chance I got. Even after I got married, when I was thirty-three, I kept saying that I wanted to have a baby and stay home and take care of it. I kept saying, 'Okay, next year, I'll quit my job and have a baby.' But next year always brought some new challenge at work or a problem that I thought I was the best person to solve. My work just got more and more important to me. It's my life. Both my husband and I are very devoted to our work, and we love it. Now, I've passed the point where I would consider having a child. No regrets, either. I'm having too much fun."

The effect of women's careers on their maternal ambivalence can be attributed to a shift in career expectations that has led many women to establish career patterns similar to those of their male peers. As we shall see later, until recently, the careers of women, and particularly those of mothers, progressed differently from men's careers.

The current maternal ambivalence displayed by women once they become heavily involved in their careers seems less puzzling when we consider that men have always been more indifferent than women about whether they needed children, partly because the physical care of children was not seen as one of their responsibilities and partly because their careers were the focal point of their lives.

Throughout most of Western history, men have not done any real fathering; they have not permitted their children to be their major or consuming interest. Apart from providing for his children financially, almost never has the care of his children taken precedence over a man's career. This is changing somewhat, though, as more men are taking advantage of changing social values to claim their paternal rights. Somewhat ironically, men are choosing to play a more prominent role in the physical and emotional nurturing of their children at the very time when women are discovering what about work has always fascinated men.

These trends suggest that neither men's seeming disinterest in parenting nor women's seeming disinterest in careers is necessarily natural, but rather, that these attitudes may result from living in a culture that forces men and women to choose between parenting and work, rather than making both roles equally accessible and rewarding to everyone—a solution that might also lead to an easier division of labor between the sexes.

Knowing that her maternal ambivalence may be the result of her natural desire to have a career, however, does not necessarily help a woman decide whether she wants to—or should—combine motherhood and work. Women sense, correctly for the most part, that motherhood in our society does not yet mix easily with a career—especially for the so-called average woman. This is something every woman of childbearing age must confront before deciding whether or not to become a mother. Evidence that this is true can be seen in the fact that many of women's work-related problems are inextricably bound up with the fact that biologically women are—potentially or in fact—mothers in addition to being workers. Women's career problems are, therefore, not the same as those of their male peers, even after allowances have been made for education and opportunities.

There are no easy answers for the woman caught in this dilemma. Furthermore, every situation must be evaluated individually. Some careers are so taxing that a woman can do little else but work. Some children are so demanding that they require a full-time mother. And, as noted earlier, there is no way to predict which kind of child—or for that matter, which kind of career—you will have. A woman can, however, examine the issue of motherhood versus career carefully before deciding either to remain childless or to combine the two.

Marriage or Children:
Which Hurts Women's Careers More?

Women's lives are complicated by the fact that they are expected to function in so many roles. Although men, too, are expected to combine a career, marriage, and fatherhood, the pressures on them in the latter two roles at least are far less than on women; in fact, many of the pressures that men could be subjected to by marriage or fatherhood are alleviated, in large part, by women. In our culture, though, a working woman is still expected to handle all her responsibilities as both mother and wife. In the majority of homes where women work, she arranges the child care and she does the housework after she comes home from work.

In addition, until recently, wives have had another responsibility, for they have also been expected to act as appendages that smoothed their husbands' paths to career success. By making the home a retreat from the competitive world of work, wives have stood by to offer their husbands whatever physical and emotional support they required at the end of a long hard day of work. Today, working wives often still fulfill this role for their husbands, while only a rare husband assumes the role of "wife" to an ambitious woman.

Perhaps these many responsibilities are why, until fairly recently, marriage and a career have appeared to be mutually exclusive for most women. Thus, few women who hoped to marry even bothered to prepare for a career. And many women who were driven toward professional achievement did not have high hopes of marrying.

For a long time, sociologists, potential husbands, and even women themselves did not believe women could successfully combine marriage and a career. To this end, women were not often even educated as well as men were until the 1950s and 1960s. Before public schools were established in the mid-nineteenth century, when those children who received an education were usually tutored at home, boys' lessons were invariably more stringent than those of girls (math and science compared to music and needlework), and girls were often released from any regular attendance in the schoolroom so they could help at home. Boys might be sent to boarding school and then on to college; a girl's education ended, or more accurately, dwindled out, around her fifteenth or sixteenth year, if not earlier. There are still vestiges of prejudice against sending a woman to college—some parents save money to send their sons to college and graduate school but deny their daughters the same educational opportunities. At any rate, a woman with a college education was for many years statistically less likely than her uneducated sisters to marry.

When sociologist Eli Ginzberg did extensive research on the lifestyles of educated women in the mid-1960s, he found that many educated women had, in fact, ruled out marriage in order to further their careers.[1] One cannot help but ask why any woman might not still want to marry even though she was educated, especially in a time when a woman who did not marry also did not have children and thus was viewed by society as twice deprived. One reason might be the totally different lives that were led by women who did marry.

Women who did not pursue careers traditionally married and had their children young. As recently as the 1950s and early 1960s women often deferred or gave up their educational plans entirely to support those of their husbands. When women with no college education did enter the work force, they could only fill low-level jobs because of their lack of education or specialized training, and did not dream of pursuing careers.

Today, though, this trend has reversed itself somewhat, and successful career women are more likely to be married than not.[2] In fact, so many women who maintain serious careers are married that social scientists now wonder whether marriage ever was the hindrance to a career that it was perceived to be. Sociologists have shifted their focus from marriage to children as the factor that limits women's career success. The fact that so much attention was ever focused on marriage as a career hindrance may have occurred only because, until fairly recently, contraception was either illegal or less reliable, so marriage almost inevitably meant children. The only sure way a woman could avoid having children was to avoid marriage. Consciously or unconsciously, many career-oriented women may have done just that—ruled out marriage so they would not have children.

In the past twenty years since the advent of the Pill and other improved forms of birth control, women have had almost total control of the number of children they bore. The current low birth rates among working women appear to support the theory that children and not marriage may have been the reason that so many women with careers in the late nineteenth and early twentieth centuries did not marry.

Research shows that married career women limit the size of their families more than any other group of women.[3] In addition, now that so many career women are married and have the means to prevent conception almost absolutely, many appear to do just that. For example, in one survey of working women in science, a career choice where much is demanded of everyone who enters the field, over one third of the women were childless, whereas only one tenth of the men were.[4] Moreover, in many fields other than science many female high achievers have remained childless, some undoubtedly by choice, among them, Emily Dickinson, Jane Austen, Susan B. Anthony, Alice Stone Blackwell, Willa Cather, Georgia O'Keeffe, Eudora Welty, Amelia Earhart. Possibly Ginzberg was only catching a glimpse of the future when he interviewed women during the 1960s who said they deliberately had chosen childlessness because they thought children would interfere with their careers.

The question that confronts women in the 1980s who have

planned careers is whether—and how—they can combine mother-hood and work.

Who Combines Motherhood and a Career?

The number of women who actually manage to combine mar-riage, children, and a very successful career is still fairly small. That these women have achieved unprecedented career success de-spite being mothers led sociologist Alice Rossi in 1973 to call them "pioneers." Women who do manage to achieve spectacular career success, according to Rossi, are "self-selected pioneers" rather than average, or traditional, women; this also led Rossi to label such women pioneers "deviants," in large part because they are still anomalies in the mainstream of American life. In a survey of 15,000 married, college-educated women, Rossi found that the typical, traditional woman grew up in the suburbs, married within a year or so after college, and wanted a suburban life that included several children. Work outside the home was something this kind of woman would consider only when her children were in school or grown. Such women also typically trained for female-dominated occupa-tions such as teaching and nursing, which were especially compatible with motherhood.[5]

By contrast, the pioneers selected an atypical life. They entered male-dominated professions, and they exhibited a high level of commitment to their careers. These women planned to have smaller than average families, were willing to delegate child rear-ing and other domestic chores to others, and said they did not relish these chores anyway. They often gave up close contacts with their families and in-laws because all their spare time was devoted to their immediate families. They saw themselves as competitive, highly energetic, and unusually good at managing their compli-cated lives. These are women who did not crumble when their child got the chicken pox and the housekeeper quit the night be-fore they were scheduled to present a paper on a new scientific breakthrough at a major conference. A pioneer woman found a way to present the paper, even if it meant leaving her ill child in someone else's care. Rossi observed, "Role deviance among women requires a profile of high physical energy and psychological toughness."[6]

Any woman who is considering combining motherhood with a career must consider whether she is endowed with the unusual quantities of energy and talent that are required to do so. For many women, the solution is to remain childless, but before a woman makes this decision, she may be helped by knowing how a working mother with normal reserves of energy exists and what problems confront her in her career as a result of being a mother.

Working Women, Working Mothers, and Careers

In general, women have more problems in achieving career success than men do. This is even more true for working mothers. Cynthia Epstein, who has written extensively on this subject, noted that no matter where women work, "like sediment in a wine bottle, they seem to settle to the bottom."[7] Of the small minority of women who do seek out professions or other demanding careers, she finds, some make it to the top, but even then, they only reach the bottom rung of the top levels to which they aspire. Almost no women sit on corporate boards, are presidents of companies, are senators or governors, or are otherwise permitted access to the upper echelons of the power structure. There is speculation over the reasons for women's lesser achievement when compared to their male peers—the way they are socialized, the lack of role models, sibling position in the family, and the training they receive have all been suggested as deterrents to women's career success— and among the many reasons given, motherhood often tops the list.

Epstein believes that, in part, women may be hindered because regardless of what they may achieve in their careers, they are always defined by their child-rearing functions. It has been documented by another researcher that women must be "overcredentialed" to be accepted as professional equals. This is true despite the fact that women who received doctorates in all subjects were brighter than men receiving doctorates and exhibited no differences in productivity or ability to work as hard as men did.[8] Epstein concluded that regardless of their career choices, women were always seen in relation to their childbearing function and child-rearing tasks. . . . The attitudes connected with the child-rearing function are those most commonly evoked in the discussion of women and work. They are often used as rationalization and justification for the status quo. What is, is regarded as necessary, natural, and just, and the effort to seek alternate solutions is therefore undermined.[9]

Working mothers do, in fact, experience a more complicated career path, choose more traditional (and perhaps less challenging) careers, and expect less from their careers than other professionals.

Although their lives may be more complicated, working women who are mothers might have an advantage over working women who are not that, until recently, has been overlooked. According to Ginzberg's research, mothers tend to have more options than other women with regard to their careers.[10] For example, they can—and are even expected to, in some circles—choose not to work for a period while rearing children full time. This has been described as a "cyclical career," one in which periods of child rearing are alternated with periods devoted to a career. Lotte Bailyn found, however, that women who leave the work force to rear children are not as likely to return as are those who continue to work even part time.[11]

Another complicating factor in the careers of mothers is that they are more likely than other workers to change careers one or more times during their working lives.[12] Although career changes have become more acceptable in recent years than in the past, when one was more or less expected to sign on with a company and stay for life, and although career switching is indicative of a new, much-needed shake-up in work patterns that ultimately will serve to accommodate working parents better than old patterns ever could, people who change careers still sometimes pay a price. This is especially true for anyone who has chosen a career in a profession such as law or corporate business where the path to the top is still rather rigidly defined. A career change also involves the time and expense of retraining as well as the time needed to establish oneself in the new field.

For many years women who trained for careers did so with an

eye on how their career choices would accommodate motherhood. Women who hoped to become mothers tended to gravitate toward nursing, teaching, or library work, because the work was thought to offer "practice" for motherhood and because the hours accommodated them when they became mothers. For example, a teacher could be home after school when her children needed her; a nurse could work from nine to three.

Although young women emerging from professional schools today often insist they can handle the demands of a career and motherhood, this rather naïve optimism is limited mostly to women in their twenties who neither participated in the women's struggle to gain equal rights nor have yet encountered the subtle and still prevalent prejudice that keeps women from the real upper echelon of power.

For many older women, the need to accept one's second or even third choice for a career has been a frustration and a lifelong burden, as this forty-year-old mother of two indicated: "I really wanted to be a doctor but I settled for being a nurse. My mother kept telling me I should be a nurse because then I could always find work but I could also be home with my children. Actually, I started out in premed, and I loved it—even the feeling that I was a woman doing men's work. But then I met Ben, and I knew I would marry him as soon as I finished college. So I switched to social work. I can't say I did it halfheartedly because I was carried away with fantasies of being a wife and mother. But I've always felt frustrated that I wasn't able to have a real career. Something has been gnawing at me all these years, and I think it is that I never did what I really wanted to do with my life."

Even among young women today, who have mostly chosen whatever career interests them, there is still a tendency to plan careers around the possibility of motherhood. Epstein found that many women who train as lawyers and physicians often decide not to practice while rearing their children.[13]

One thirty-five-year-old woman, a recent medical school graduate, who was heavily in debt for her education, rejected several lucrative offers to enter private practice and instead entered the much lower-paying field of medical research because she was offered a job where her work would make few demands on her outside regular office hours and would thus allow her to juggle a career and children.

Another woman, who graduated at the top of her law school class, went to work for a corporation but only for a year or two. She discussed her future plans, saying, "I figure I'll do this for a couple of years, and then I'll move into public service, working for the government. I know it won't be as much fun or as stimulating as corporate law—it's a bureaucracy, after all. But it also means I can take time off to have children. You can't do that when you're bucking for partner."

Less is also expected professionally of mothers than of their colleagues, male or female, who do not shoulder the responsibilities of children.

Ginzberg found that having children had one of two effects on a woman's professional life. It could enable her to drop her career, or it could force her to drop it.[14] Particularly—and understandably— in the immediate post-World War II years up until the 1960s, women tended to let motherhood take precedence over their careers, such as they were, and dropped them. Today, by contrast, few women plan to give up their careers for motherhood, so the question really comes down to whether these women will be forced to do so.

Almost every woman who tries to combine motherhood and a serious career today quickly learns that society expects her work to take a back seat to motherhood, no matter how urgent or important her work may be. In most people's eyes, motherhood is her primary role. Because of the way they are reared, most women themselves also put motherhood first, no matter how much of a pull work has on them. For many women, this results in serious role conflict. Epstein noted that any woman who attempts to combine a career and motherhood will wage a constant inner battle over this:

> Should she conform to the demands imposed on her because she is a mother or wife, or should she give priority to those demands which come as a result of being a doctor or scientist? What must she do when, as often occurs, the two conflict?

The role strain experienced by the woman professional can easily become constant and enervating, aggravated by the ambiguity that makes necessary a new decision for each minor conflict, and by the often conflicting positions taken by other people in her role network.[15]

The conflict for a working woman often begins as soon as she announces her pregnancy to her supervisor. Both she and her employer or supervisor almost immediately begin to concern themselves with new working arrangements that will be required after she has a child. Will she continue to work? If so, will she be able to work at the same pace? Will she be unable, for example, to travel? Will her concentration be reduced? Will more of her attention be directed toward her child than her job? Will she have to take days off if her child is sick or to attend school functions? These and many other questions run through her head and her boss's head.

But the most pressing problem for both is how much time she will want off before and immediately after the child is born. The answer is not only highly variable, depending upon the type of work the woman is engaged in, the woman, and the child, but also uncertain since most women do not realistically know how much time off they will want until they have had the child. The longer a woman takes off, though, the less likely she is to return to that job and that career. Some women take off only a few weeks or months while others find they want several years off. Some women plan for six weeks and take six years.

Even women who are self-employed have to gauge how much time they will need away from their work when they become mothers. Peggy, age thirty, the mother of a four-month-old daughter, had worked for eight years to establish herself as a writer before getting pregnant. She recalled how unrealistically she had calculated the amount of time her child would consume: "I had tried to be realistic about my work. People said I would need three, maybe six, months off, but I kept saying, oh, no, I'll work the next week. . . . After my daughter was born, every day, every week, for months I would think it was time to get on with my work, but it was too much to work and take care of her, too. Maybe it was my hormones—I don't know—but I felt as if my head had been cut off, and I was just a body. I took months to get back to my work."

Sandra, age thirty-four, who did return to work when her son was a month old, said the change in her life was enormous and frighteningly unpredictable. She recalled, "Suddenly, my well-ordered life became a series of maintenance tasks. I wanted to keep my career, but now I was also a mother and I was still a wife. Believe me, all three are full-time jobs. It was so much harder to work and have a baby than I ever imagined."

Asked if life might not have been easier if she had given up her work, she said, "Of course it would have been, but I won't do that. I need my work for my self-respect." She added, "I love my son, and I wouldn't trade him for anything in the world, but I know now that considering how important my work is to me, I would have been better off not having any children."

While the job may be waiting for the woman who takes a short maternity leave, a leave of any length can hurt her career in many ways. In many fields—science, medicine, law, journalism—a key employee's absence for more than a few weeks may be enough to leave that person behind professionally for months or years. The work is there when the woman returns, but she may never catch up, particularly if she has been gone for months or years.

Women who stay out for months or years often try to maintain their professional skills, but this effort more frequently fades in the face of the time and effort that are required to care for a baby. As Peggy said, she had no time for writing. Certainly, a stockbroker, a banker, a lawyer, and a salesperson would probably not even have a way to maintain her skills and contacts.

Sometimes, the only thing that can be maintained is the illusion of keeping up, and in many fields that is indeed an illusion. A physicist who took off six months with her first child said, "The information changes so fast in my branch of physics that I was behind a month after I left. I had to take two courses to refresh myself before I could go back to work. With my second child, it was even harder." This is true to greater or lesser degrees in most professions and for many nonprofessional jobs as well.

Mothers are also penalized when they take long maternity leaves in ways that are not so measurable. Women, who often start their careers earning less than men and in positions of less power, lose out on whatever wages and raises they would normally have received if they had worked steadily. Also hard to measure is the cost to women of falling so far behind their peers. These losses are never really made up. As Epstein noted, many employers would view such losses as part of the price women pay to work and be mothers.

Timing the Baby:
When Is It Right for Your Career?

In the 1950s and 1960s women were advised to have their babies young so they could return to work or start their careers after their children were in school. But these women soon found they could not establish themselves in careers when they started fifteen years later than everyone else. The men and childless women who had graduated at the same time were fifteen irretrievable years ahead of these women, and the young college graduates with whom they also competed for jobs offered skills that were fresher and more up-to-date.

Today, women tend to postpone having children until they have gotten their educations and established themselves in careers. Even so, many of these women still find themselves perplexed about when to fit a baby into their careers. Phyllis, now thirty-six and right where she wants to be in her career as a commodities broker, commented, "I know it's time to have a baby, if I'm ever going to, but I've worked ten years to build up my client list, and it won't be there if I leave for a year or six months or even a month."

Nancy, age thirty-three, a lawyer who just made junior partner, said, "Everyone says don't have a baby until you've finished law school, gotten through the first five years at a law firm, made junior partner, and so on. So I've done all those things, but there has been no letup in my work or in my desire to work. The longer I wait, the harder it gets to decide to take time off to have a baby. When is the best time? How am I supposed to know when it strikes?"

The Pressure to Reproduce

The timing of an established professional woman's children is also a subject of concern to others. Although they do so for different reasons, a woman's mother, husband, and employer all may apply pressure on her to have a baby if she is going to.

For example, a mother who is undergoing some feelings of jeal-

ousy or competition with her daughter may urge her into motherhood. Another mother whose life was devoted to her children may
not feel she can compete with or, for that matter, relate to her
daughter as an adult until they have both experienced motherhood.
A mother who really wanted a career but had children instead may
resent her daughter's success and step up the pressure on her at
those times when the daughter is rewarded for her work. The
reasons that mothers urge daughters into motherhood are varied
and complex.

Jill, a forty-year-old childless banker, said that just when her career escalated, so did the pressure from her mother and mother-in-
law on her to get pregnant: "When I was about thirty-four I was
offered a position in the international department—something I
had always wanted. That was when my husband and I decided not
to have any children. He didn't care one way or the other, and my
work meant a lot to me. So I was sterilized. We did this quietly,
not even telling our parents at the time.

"Somehow, both mothers sensed what this promotion had meant
to me. They knew I had pretty much resolved my ambivalence
over whether to be a mother, except maybe they each thought they
had one more chance at talking me into it. The pressure from both
sides was amazing. And it only let up when I finally told both
mothers what I had done.

"Now they treat me completely differently, almost as if I'm one
of the men in the family. I don't think either woman knows how to
relate to me since I'm not a mother. At family dinners the women—
that is, the mothers—gather in the kitchen and talk about children,
of course. I stay in the living room and talk business with the men.
Actually I don't mind, except I'm a little hurt sometimes that they
don't make any effort to include me."

Timing a Baby to His Career

Some women find their husbands are the ones who apply the
pressure to have a baby. At the same time that a woman's career is
taking off, her husband's career usually is, too, with the result that
he may feel more confident than he has in the past about other
areas of his life. Many people do not let themselves think about

some areas of their lives—personal relationships and family life being two of the more common areas that frequently are dispatched to the subconscious at certain stages of life—until they have achieved a certain amount of career recognition. Thus, it is not surprising that many men pressure their wives to become pregnant when their own careers become more settled. Partly, they may do this because they do finally feel financially established enough to start a family, but this may also be a way to lessen the potential for career competition between spouses.

One now divorced man said, "My wife and I were both professionals, I in medicine and she in law. Although we weren't direct competitors, I think we did compete on many levels. I wasn't a traditional husband and consciously chose not to have a traditional marriage, but I increasingly resented that whenever I talked about a problem at work, she came right back with a problem she had. My mother never did that to my father. I know this is something I have to resolve, because I don't want a woman who stays home all day and waits for me to come home, but I would also be lying if I didn't admit that it's a struggle for me to be more liberated in my marriage than my parents were. And while my second wife has a career, she is not so dedicated to it as my first wife was to hers. We're going to have children. I suppose that was part of my subconscious solution."

A woman who holds an executive position in retailing said, "I thought Jack and I had sorted everything out about children. We weren't going to have any. But then his career took off, and he earned a lot of money and was going to earn even more, and suddenly, he wanted children. I was working because I loved my work; he thought I was working because we needed the money. Now that he could afford to support me, as he put it, and also a child, that was what he wanted to do. It broke up our marriage. It's funny, though, I don't hold him responsible. I honestly don't think he knew what he wanted or how badly he would want a child until he got a certain degree of security. I can't blame him for that."

The Pain of Potential Motherhood

A woman's boss also may pressure her to reproduce. Fully supportive as a boss or mentor may be of a woman's career, he also may harbor fears that he will lose someone in whom he has invested time and energy. Thus, he may encourage a woman to have children as a means of testing her real intentions. A woman who has announced that she plans to remain childless is usually not believed and may continue to be subjected by her boss to questions about when she plans to have a baby. A boss's anxiety often soars when he is about to promote a woman or give her some special recognition or assignment.

Gail, at age thirty-eight, assumed she was about to be named as her boss's successor in an important job when she found herself without support she had taken for granted. She recalled, "I thought he would recommend me. After all, he had been grooming me for the job for years, and we had talked about it. But when it was time to do so, he took me aside and told me I should go have babies, that now was no time to pursue my career and miss out on something like motherhood. This came from a man whom I had constantly reassured of my intentions to remain childless. He didn't even have anyone else to recommend, and the company eventually went outside to replace him. I think he got cold feet, and thought he would look silly if he recommended me for the job and then I got pregnant."

Gail's case is not that unusual. She got hurt by a prevalent cultural belief that all women really want to be mothers, no matter that they may say otherwise. Some people even believe that a woman who does not want to be a mother is abnormal. Many people think childless women do not know their own minds or feelings, that they will eventually succumb to motherhood.

Judith, age twenty-six, an account executive in a public relations firm, experienced something similar to Gail when her mentor of many years withdrew his support. She said, "Believe it or not, the issue was motherhood. He simply didn't believe me when I said I never planned to have children. Whenever we would have drinks after work, he would get around to the subject of children, how it was abnormal not to have them, how I must really want to be a mother. At the same time, he really respected my work and wanted to use my mind for his projects. I was in a no-win situation. If I had a child, then I couldn't be counted on to do my work or to be as hard-driven as I was before I became a mother. But if I didn't have a child, then there was something wrong, abnormal, with me, and maybe I was still too flaky to be taken seriously or promoted. After he stopped helping me, I got another job. I would like to say that this is less of an issue now, and it is in many ways, but I still think the people I work with are waiting for me to have a baby. Last year, a man who had less experience than I did was promoted over me. I think I know what that's about."

Unfortunately, there are no easy answers for the woman who chooses to combine motherhood and a career except to make her aware of the pitfalls she is liable to encounter. As for the woman who has decided on childlessness, until it becomes more acceptable, if many women's experiences are typical, she still may have trouble with her career because of her potential for motherhood. Since few women are eager to reveal intimate details at work— such as the fact, for example, that they may have been sterilized (and even fewer women are willing to close the door so permanently on motherhood)—the problems a woman has at work over her potential to mother may be ongoing for many years.

The Ultimate Question: Is Motherhood a Woman's Most Creative Act?

Now that women do have a choice to make about motherhood, and now that so many are seeing the possibility of fulfilling themselves through many kinds of creative career work, many women are questioning how creative motherhood and, for that matter, how creative work is—and whether the two must always exist in conflict. Most women who work outside their homes at traditional and often professional jobs tend to see their work and motherhood in terms of conflict. Not too surprisingly, women who work at home and in the arts are more likely to see motherhood as something that can enhance their creativity. One artist said, "I think of my work and motherhood as a piece. Both require my energy, and both are creative. I think I could fulfill my creative efforts through motherhood, but right now, I feel more creative because of my painting. And I know that my supply of energy is not unlimited. What I take for one part of my life or activity reduces what I have left for another. I suppose I'll always feel conflicted over this, and I also think it's a special problem that creative women have. Sometimes

I'm jealous of women who keep their lives simple. They always knew they wanted to be mothers, and they are mothers. But this is silly envy, because I can't do anything about it. I can't change what I am, and right now that is a woman who is more interested in artistic creativity than in motherhood."

Peggy, the writer we met earlier, saw her infant daughter as a catalyst for her creative energy: "I plan to use my motherhood in my writing. Sometimes I think I will write about my daughter. I've already written an article about how hard it is to be a mother and about the problems I had accepting motherhood. I had a pediatrician who asked me what I do. When I said, 'I'm a writer,' she said, 'Oh, you'll see what this is going to do to your writing.' It's too early to tell though, but I thought she was encouraging. I think anything that moves you very deeply, it's creative—in that sense, I view motherhood as being creative and helpful to me in my own creative life."

For other women, motherhood remains the ultimate creative act —even for this twenty-eight-year-old woman who says she will never have children: "Of course, I think it is the most creative thing a woman can do. To give birth and then nurture and care for a child is very special work. I even think women have a maternal instinct that makes them want to do this, but I also don't think a woman suffers if she doesn't become a mother, especially today, when there are so many things women can do with their lives. I do get twinges when I look at little babies sometimes, but mostly I think motherhood is not for me. I know I can live my whole life without having children because my work is so important to me."

Talk of creativity, careers, and motherhood is really an expression of women's concern over the possibilities of their lives today. But it is also a way of exploring another subject of deep concern to them: regrets. Will there perhaps be regrets later in life over not having chosen motherhood? Is motherhood women's ultimate creative act, something that every woman should if possible experience in order to feel totally female?

Unfortunately, there is really only one possible response to women who wonder if they will be missing something if they do not become mothers, and that is that no one really knows, and no one can predict, how any one woman will feel years later over her decision. Of the middle-aged and older women interviewed for this

book, not one expressed serious misgivings over not having had
children, and many had found many pluses about their childless
lives. Some of the middle-aged women had deliberately decided
not to have children, and the older ones in their sixties through
their eighties felt they had been physically unable to do so. (The
reader should recall, too, that few women in these age groups were
interviewed for this book.) However, just as no one can predict
whether a woman will experience deep regret or suffer from
depression or other emotional problems as a result of not having
had a child, no one can predict what resentments a woman will
have if she chooses motherhood ambivalently when she really
wants a career.

6.
MOM IN THE WORKPLACE: A REALISTIC GOAL?

The plight of working mothers today cannot have gone unnoticed by any woman who is weighing whether she, too, wants to jump into a life that looks so difficult. Some women feel that their careers, or sometimes even a marriage that is less stable than it might be, are stumbling blocks to having children, but they also note that these stumbling blocks could be removed or pushed aside more easily if women were assured of the right kind of social support—the kind that would represent a genuine change in attitude toward women—when they chose to combine marriage, careers, and children. At present this kind of social support is sorely lacking for all but a highly elite group of women who can afford to replace themselves in the home.

Most obviously, employers have done little to accommodate working mothers or even to encourage them. Suggestions of flexible working hours or shared jobs—ways of employing working mothers and helping them juggle their multiroled lives—have failed to arouse either enthusiasm or action on the part of employers. Few corporations have expressed any intentions of providing on-premises day care, a solution that has worked to the advantage of both employers and women in some countries. Nor do corporations show much interest in contributing funds to community day-care centers. In addition, neither local nor federal government has shown much interest in either prodding employers or providing incentives that might spur them into action. Working mothers, who are often handicapped from the start by prejudice against any mother who works for other than economic reasons, have had to struggle for every benefit they have obtained: paid maternity leave, the right to return to the same job, the freedom to take time off when needed to care for their children.

Women do not get much more help on the domestic front, either. Although there were optimistic signs a few years ago that marriages were changing—that is, becoming more egalitarian—this has not really happened and women who work continue to shoulder most of the child care and domestic responsibility.

Finally, although this is something that no one could prevent, the way Americans live has changed over the past forty years so much that women generally can no longer count on the emotional and physical support that existed for generations among families and in neighborhoods. The very special kind of informal support network, consisting of family and neighbors, that was often the mainstay of a young mother's life is almost nonexistent today.

Although these may seem to be three disparate factors—lack of support from employers, from family, and from friends—they are actually related. All three are symptoms of a social system that does not entirely welcome or comfortably accommodate women who combine motherhood and work.

One thirty-three-year-old woman thought the lack of social support was the single most important reason for her decision to remain childless: "I know that several generations from now women will get the support they need, and combining work and motherhood won't pose the problems it does today. For right now, today, with regard to my life, it's too much of a hassle. I would have to spend all my time, to say nothing of most of my income, arranging for child care. And I do think a baby would hurt my career. My employer would not be nice about giving me time off, even to take care of a sick child. Well, he might be nice on the surface, but underneath it all, he would question how dedicated I was to my job. These are battles I would have to fight for years. I keep that in mind whenever I start to get carried away with how cute little babies are."

Another woman, forty-five years old and childless, said, "My husband is of the generation that doesn't believe in helping around the house, or, for that matter, in the nursery. We talked for a long time about having a baby, and he said it was fine with him, I should go ahead and do it, but I shouldn't count on him for any help. I see women who work—younger women, mostly—in marriages where the husband does help, but such men seem to be rare. I blame our social system or our value system or whatever for that. Men are just brought up believing they don't have to help with these matters. It's accepted in our culture that they won't. I don't even blame my husband personally since I have to admit that I have played along with it in our marriage."

Another woman, twenty-eight years old and unsure about whether she can juggle a career and children, also felt that the lack of social support would hinder her if she decided to have a baby: "What keeps me from finally having children aren't the things I can control, like getting my husband to help with child care or even getting child care, for that matter. It's the attitude toward mothers who work—the way everyone seems to be waiting for them to fall on their faces. I won't mind the extra time and money that will be needed to take a child to day care, but I'll hate having to face an employer who basically thinks it's wrong to put a little child in day care. It's only an attitude, I know, but attitudes can hurt. I don't think things like this will change until the entire social system changes."

And until the entire social system does change, it is something that ambivalent women may want to consider when weighing child-lessness and motherhood. How important this kind of support is depends upon the individual woman, but any woman who is con-sidering adding motherhood to a career, or even to a marriage that is not all it might be, should examine not only what her life will be like without children, which has mostly been the topic of the pre-ceding chapters, but also what her life will be like if she decides to go ahead and have a child, which is described in the following pages. Motherhood, of course, always has its rewards, but for some ambivalent women, the rewards may not be enough if the sacrifices turn out to be too great. Much of the information and examples that follow describe motherhood in a fairly bad light. They also deal with situations that individual women may not be able to control or change to any large degree. Despite this, this chapter is meant to educate, not to warn.

The New Social Isolation

Women today must cope with a new kind of social isolation that can mostly be ascribed to the times in which they live. Prior to World War II, a young middle-class mother, who was likely to be a homemaker, could assume she would receive a certain amount of physical and emotional support from her own mother or mother-in-law, sisters, and perhaps a maiden aunt, in addition to friendly neighbors who were often themselves young mothers. Such persons were not only willing to help, but, because they lived nearby, they were available to help. Obviously, such a network would be especially valuable to working mothers today. A mother or sister, if nonworking, could take over when a child was ill or needed someone to attend a school function. Instead of taking a child to day care, perhaps a nonworking friend would lend a hand. Yet in an era when so many women could benefit from arrangements like this, the system is rapidly disappearing. Today, the mother and sisters of a working mother are themselves often employed, and if they are not, they often do not live nearby, or even in the same community, anymore.

The fact that Americans now move on the average every five years has contributed to another kind of isolation for young mothers—one that is psychological as well as physical. Family members may see each other only once or twice a year, and then under the kinds of pressure that build up around holidays or during a long visit. Such is the isolation of modern life that a woman who becomes a mother often finds she has no other woman who is already a part of her life with whom to share the immediate joys and pains of motherhood. Instead, she must begin to seek out the company of other mothers. The kind of informal camaraderie that exists among mothers everywhere is not hard to join, but such friendships, while invaluable in one sense, are often based on little more than the common experience of motherhood and are rarely a replacement for sharing the experience with mothers, sisters, and old friends.

Apart from the isolation that comes from living hundreds of miles from family and old friends, the fact that many couples choose, or are forced by economics and the need for more space, to move to the suburbs when they start a family creates yet another set of potential problems for the new mother. The typical suburban housewife may find herself isolated, even if she does not work outside her home, in a way that would have seemed strange to her grandmother or mother.

Prior to the mushrooming of the suburbs, many families lived in houses or apartments situated in well-defined neighborhoods. A large part of a woman's day could be spent in the company of other neighborhood women if she so desired. Women gathered at the local laundromat or over backyard fences or chatted when they met in local stores; they walked their children at the same time of day in the neighborhood park. For that matter, a woman could easily attract visitors merely by taking an afternoon break on the front porch or putting fresh-baked pies to cool on a windowsill. Such gestures were invariably considered an invitation for company.

Today suburban women typically live in apartments or detached homes that are centrally cooled and heated and rarely, if ever, open to the neighborhood. When a suburban woman leaves her detached house, she does not walk out into the neighborhood, but rather, she goes directly into a garage and then drives away in her car, thus further reducing the possibility of even a chance encounter with a neighbor.

Any woman who works, as more than half of all mothers now do, may find her life in the neighborhood, whether it is suburban or urban, even more diminished, if that is possible. She may bump into—and barely recognize—her neighbors at a school function or a meeting of the homeowners' association or block association. More often, she does not have time to attend such functions, and she would not recognize her neighbors if she met them on the street.

Lacking familial support and also lacking a neighborhood network, to whom does the working mother turn for the kind of support and advice that women have counted on from one another for so many generations? How does she find the time to build friendships with other women? The answer is, mostly, that she does not.

Like most people who work, women tend to find their friends among their co-workers, but a working mother may encounter special problems even here. Although much has been written in recent years about networks for women, these are, for the most part, artificially structured groups, especially when compared to the kind of informal ties that formerly existed among relatives and neighbors. In addition, these networks are not designed to support working mothers, but rather, to help women handle their professional lives. Besides, the working mother often has as little time for this kind of socializing as for any other kind. In fact, after a woman has a child and her schedule becomes more crowded, her professional friendships are often the first thing to go. Even personal friendships sometimes suffer. A working mother typically rushes from work to home so she can spend her few precious free hours taking care of her family. Needless to say, there is no time to build new friendships, either.

One woman sadly recalled an encounter that had happened to her when a woman made an overture toward friendship: "I recently became friends with a new woman at work—my first real friend in five years. She had just moved from another city, and since I had moved several times since I had gotten married, I knew she must be a little lonely. She is also single, so that must have made moving harder still. We started having lunch regularly— something I have not even allowed myself to do very often since my son was born. I usually rush around and do errands on my lunch hour so I can spend the evening with my family. Finally, this woman asked me if I would like to go to a movie or play with her some night. I felt awful that I had to tell her that I couldn't because I feel obligated to spend all my free time with my family. I felt really bad. I think I needed that friendship even more than she did. But my life just doesn't seem to be set up to leave me time for friendship with other women."

Friendships too often become a smaller rather than a greater source of personal support for the working mother, nor do they serve as a kind of reality check on her multiroled life-style. If they did, she might learn that her problems are shared by other working mothers, and she might have the solace and advice of other women in her situation.

The Superwoman Syndrome

The reason that most working mothers do not feel they can make the time for something so important as friendships with other

women can be found in how they function at home. Although
many people today feel their lives are complicated and overbur-
dened, no one's life is more so than that of the working mother. Increasingly, working mothers are falling victim to what has been
dubbed the "Superwoman" syndrome.

According to Caryl Rivers, Rosalind Barnett, and Grace Baruch,
authors of a book titled *Beyond Sugar and Spice: How Women
Grow, Learn, and Thrive,* Superwoman is "the executive who is a
whiz from nine to five and dashes home to whip up a marvelous
soufflé and read fairy tales to the kids."[1] Largely a creation of the
media, she is reminiscent of the woman who, in one television perfume advertisement, assumed a braggadocio stance and announced
that she could bring home the bacon *and* fry it. The woman in the
ad somehow manages to do everything demanded of her as a
housewife and mother, while still finding the time to douse herself
with perfume and slip into something sexy to greet her man. And
one imagines that she runs an equally tight ship at the office. Even
though few do it with the style of the woman in the ad, more and
more women find themselves assuming the role of Superwoman;
most do so without first contemplating some of the grittier realities
of her life that never make it to the television screen.

To no one's surprise but her own, Superwoman often fails to
manage with quite the aplomb of the media-spawned ideal. In fact,
the darker side of Superwoman is a sense of personal failure and
denigration that many women experience when they think they are
not managing their elaborate juggling act as well as they might.

There is little reason, however, for Superwoman to be successful;
her burdens would be too much for practically anyone. And as we
shall see, she not only does not get much help, but she does not ask
for much help, either.

Superwoman's Modus Operandi

Most people picture the working mother as a highly organized
domestic manager. They also assume that she, her husband, and
her children all share equally in household chores and maintenance. But this is hardly the case. Most of this work still falls primarily on the woman's shoulders. A survey of twelve countries
showed that most working mothers are busier than most heads of

state.[2] Being responsible for running the family, working mothers have to do the bulk of the chauffeuring, laundering, and dishwashing (3,500 dishes per one month for a family of four, by one estimate), as well as the nurturing of children and the arranging of the family's social life.[3]

In addition, research has shown that working mothers tend to overcompensate with their husbands, while they are oversolicitous of their children. For example, although they request and get more help from their husbands than do nonworking wives, working mothers, unable perhaps to erase totally the guilt they feel over working, tend to assign their husbands easy or pleasurable tasks while reserving the ongoing, mundane jobs for themselves. In child care, men feed, bathe, and tell stories, but they do not often do these things regularly, nor do they assume ongoing responsibilities for the child such as chauffeuring, clothes shopping, or taking complete physical care of the child for a period of time.[4] They also typically do one-shot housekeeping tasks such as waxing a floor or washing windows rather than taking responsibility for the family laundry or grocery shopping.

Child care traditionally has been viewed as women's work, and there are no signs that this is changing, even though half of all mothers with preschool age children now work. One woman notes that she even runs the house, in absentia, when she travels on business: "I stock the refrigerator with food, plan their meals, and arrange for child care for those times when my husband isn't around. Whoever heard of a man making similar preparations for a business trip he was going to take?"

Working mothers also do not usually ask their children to do any more chores than nonworking mothers do, and many ask their children to do less, as if by way of apology for not being full-time mothers. One mother explains, "My child didn't ask to have a working mother, and I don't see why he should pay a special price for it." Another mother said, "I just don't have the heart to ask my daughter to do more when I do less as a mother than other mothers do. I miss all her school functions because I work."

Because so much of their time and energy is required to maintain a home, many working mothers are unable to spend as much time as they might like with their children. Mothering, or at least the truly pleasurable part of it, frequently gets short shrift in the face of the effort needed to keep a house clean, get to the dry cleaner before it closes, and pick up the car at the garage.

Families with two working parents often spend far less time together than they might like to. One working mother of a seven-year-old son said, "When I come home from work at night, I would often like to have a drink with my husband, but what do I do? I listen to my son discuss his day or practice the piano. And I do that because I only get to spend about an hour and a half a day like that with him. We even do all our errands together as a family on Saturdays even though it would be more efficient to split up because we have more time together that way."

Working Mothers' Problems on the Job

If working mothers have problems at home, they often encounter other kinds of problems on the job. Mostly, these have to do with attitudes and expectations. Although a working mother's job may be of the utmost importance to her, expectations may not be the same for her as for other women, to the detriment of her career. Often, standards are lowered for mothers, whether they want or need them to be. Cynthia Epstein wrote:

> The "new" woman is a perfectly balanced person who does a little of everything—a little writing and research; a little gourmet cooking; a little loving; a little mothering. But nowhere is she expected to rise to the top of her profession.[5]

If this appears to let a working mother off the hook by recognizing how busy she is, it is also descriptive of a somewhat negative attitude that employers too often take toward working mothers. In other words, not only is the working mother not expected to rise to the top, but she is also not encouraged, prompted, or otherwise helped to do so. Employers and society tend to maintain an attitude toward working mothers that consists of admiring them only so long as they do not forget that they are first and foremost mothers.

Epstein remarked that "for a woman, sex status is primary and pivotal, and it invariably determines much of the course of her life, especially because of the rigid cultural definitions which limit the range of other statuses she may acquire."[6] In addition to slowing down a working mother's career, such attitudes serve to distance her from her colleagues, her boss, and even the society in which she lives.

Sometimes the attitude toward working mothers is even harsher and more complicated than that indicated by simply lowering expectations for her. Only a rare working mother has not at one time or another run head on into the kind of guilt-provoking disapproval that is specifically reserved for a mother who is not poverty-stricken yet nonetheless chooses to work. Working mothers have been blamed for everything from the high unemployment and divorce rates to juvenile delinquency to the destruction of family life. And although working mothers are in vogue at the moment, the tide could easily turn against them as it has done in the past, most notably when President Theodore Roosevelt mounted a vociferous campaign in the early 1900s against the declining birth rate among white, middle-class women.

If public opinion were to turn against working mothers, it would matter little that most experts now recognize that women need to work for their self-esteem. For example, the authors of *Beyond Sugar and Spice* wrote: "One of the key ingredients for well-being in our society—in any society, for that matter—is access to the means of economic survival. Without that, almost everything in your life comes tumbling down around your head."[7] Research has also shown that women who work full time have more power at home than those who work part time or not at all.[8] Nevertheless, or perhaps even partly because of this, society periodically lashes out at the working mother just as it does at the childless woman. And even when it does not, there is a continued resistance toward accepting her as a full equal in the workplace—let alone wholeheartedly supporting her endeavor to combine motherhood and work.

Apart from the emotional and psychological support that would be helpful, physical support is also lacking. Although obtaining adequate child care is a working mother's biggest worry, employers offer little assistance in this area. Despite the prevalent feeling even among women that employers have grown more sensitive to their wants and needs, a recent survey revealed that only 1 of 309 companies contacted provided on-premises day-care facilities.[9] Cost is the reason, say employers, shaking their heads sympathetically because they have learned that harried working mothers also consider sympathy to be a form of reward. Yet the Zale Company, which set up a child-care center at its headquarters, spent only $185,000 to do so, and contributes only $10,000 a year toward its upkeep.[10]

Furthermore, despite the subtle and not so subtle tax incentives to have children, the working mother got no breaks at all until recently, and even now, gets only minimal aid in the form of tax relief. Only in the last few years have working mothers even been able to deduct child care. In 1983, the deduction was a maximum of 30 percent of child-care expenses for those who earned $10,000 or less, declining to a cutoff of 20 percent for anyone earning more than $28,000 a year. The average child-care deduction is about $850, less than a third the cost of leaving a preschool child with a caretaker who charges a rock-bottom rate of $60 per week. The federal funding that does exist for child-care centers is constantly in jeopardy from budget cuts, and even the deduction for child care, several tax experts warned, cannot be viewed as permanent.

Many middle-class women shy away from day care for their children anyway because so many facilities are geared to low-income families and are often considered inadequate by middle-class standards. Thirty million children in the United States today have working parents, but the Work in America Institute, Inc., estimates that as many as 5 million children are inadequately cared for while their parents work.[11]

Ironically, the years when a woman is most likely to be having children are also the years when she is least likely to earn enough to pay for child care. And while young professional men and women often find it easy to borrow money to establish themselves in business or law or medical practice, no one ever heard of a bank lending a woman money to pay for child care so she could establish herself in a career. According to one study, women do not even use scholarship or stipend money to obtain child care that will enable them to do their academic work.

When working women push for day care, flexible working hours, or shared jobs—any of the several things that have been suggested as ways to ease the burden on working mothers—they are frequently made to feel guiltier still. Isn't it enough that women have jobs, jobs that are, in fact, often falsely viewed as unnecessary except to bolster women's sense of self-esteem, the employers and many others ask, without demanding these other things, too? If women want to have children, the message goes, as blatantly as skywriting, then they should stay home and take care of them.

Given all these deterrents, it is no wonder that trying to be Superwoman takes its toll on women. But in addition to the obvious costs to women's pocketbooks and psyches, there are two other signs that point to the fact that all may not be well with working mothers. For some time, experts predicted that working women would lose their mysterious immunity to coronary disease once they had jobs that were as demanding as those of men. The warning then appeared to come true, with one unexplained qualification: a recent study showed that single working women were not so likely as married working women to suffer from coronary disease. This finding puzzled researchers because they found that as a group, married working women experienced no special stresses that made them more susceptible to coronary disease. But the mystery was solved when they further found that the subgroup of working *mothers* statistically appeared to be at greater risk.[12]

Another sign that may indicate there are special stresses to which working mothers are subjected is the increased level of conflict between work and family that workers now report. In 1960 only 1 percent of workers reported feeling any conflict between work and family; by 1970 that figure had risen to 25 percent.[13] Although this study does not specify how many of these workers were women, the dramatic rise in conflict over family versus work took place at the same time that large numbers of women entered the work force. Carolyn Elliott, author of a recent article titled "The Superwoman Phenomenon," wrote that the result of having a working mother in the home was "often that everyone in the family does well except for the mother: Standards of housework don't decline, community involvement changes but is still sustained—only the mother gets less sleep."[14]

❀

Unfortunately for some women, even though most segments of society have made the transition into the post-industrial age, the organization of family life still is molded in a traditional shape that came into being over 150 years ago when industrialization took the world by storm. While this outdated social system is injurious to working mothers today, its highest toll will still be reserved for the millions of women who are presently experiencing maternal ambivalence—who find themselves unable to decide whether or not to become mothers in a world that offers them so little real social support.

There is, for the most part, no way to categorize neatly the reasons that women are experiencing so much ambivalence; they vary with the individual woman, and women themselves are rarely able to attribute their childlessness to any one cause. But one thing is certain: apart from the rational, well-thought-out reasons of many women who will choose childlessness, some others will remain childless not out of any deep-seated personal need but because their culture makes it so extremely difficult for them to combine motherhood with meaningful work.

7.
FEMINISM AND THE POLITICS OF CHILDLESSNESS

The origins of universal motherhood—that is, the notion that every woman should be a mother—are to be found in the women's movement, and ironically, here, too, are to be found the origins of past and present views about childlessness. During the two waves of feminist activity that have swept the United States—the first having begun in the 1840s and 1850s and culminated in 1920 when women were granted suffrage and the second having begun in the early 1960s and continued even today—motherhood has been a pivotal issue in the struggle to define women's role in society. And only by understanding how motherhood has been used to define women's role can the present position of the mainstream women's movement on childlessness be seen in its proper context.

In one sense, childlessness and motherhood are opposite but not necessarily opposing sides of the same issue: women's right to reproductive freedom. The way the feminist movements have dealt with childlessness is important because only through the kind of social changes that have been won by feminists can women hope to obtain and secure their reproductive freedom.

The reasons that childlessness has been played down and childless women even ostracized are strategic as well as historical. Strategically, feminists, like other reformers, have had to work within their culture and, perhaps more important, they have had to respond to historical events they have not initiated or, for that matter, even anticipated. For example, in the early 1900s, opponents of women's rights unexpectedly raised the specter of a lowered birth rate as a reason to deny women expanded rights. If women developed strong interests outside of motherhood, the opponents argued, they would soon lose all interest in having babies, and the birth rate would fall, thus harming all of society. As a response, the early feminists' strategy was to rally around motherhood, insisting that their roles as mothers was the most important reason to grant them suffrage. The right to vote was viewed as a sign of respect toward women that would carry over into their roles as mothers and would make women better mothers. The result was that early feminists proclaimed their support of motherhood at the expense of offering support to women who might either have preferred to remain childless or who at least wanted the option to do so. The over-emphasis on motherhood has persisted until the present.

Perhaps this is why so many childless women today do not feel any special tie to the women's movement, or if they are feminists, why they find themselves critical of this aspect of the movement. While some of the more radical feminist groups have proposed that women stop bearing children as a protest against their cultural oppression, mainstream feminism has mostly rejected this idea and has instead sought ways that women could combine motherhood with meaningful professional work.

Speaking of feminism, one woman commented, "I don't even associate my decision to be childless with the women's movement. It's simply not a political decision for me. It's a personal one, a very personal one."

Another woman said, "Although I am a feminist, I don't think the feminists have done enough to support women's right to reproductive freedom. Why don't feminists say it's okay not to have children? Why don't they help women make this decision? Or why don't they do it more actively? I do think my decision not to have children is personal, but I could use some reinforcement, and the logical source of that reinforcement would be, I think, the women's movement."

Of course, many ambivalent and childless women also do not go out of their way to align themselves with the women's movement because, while not the most traditional of groups by virtue of their demographic characteristics (they are mostly urban dwellers and hold typically urban liberal values), these women are also not in any sense a radical group. Nor, for that matter, could they even be said to be a particularly untraditional group. For almost all women, the decision to remain childless is personal and is not based on any underlying political or social belief. It is even doubtful that "childless women" per se can be classified as a group at all, so varied are their reasons for choosing childlessness.

As for feminists' historical stance, it would have been futile for any woman to confront the women's movement with a demand that childlessness be treated as a matter of great importance when the feminists' strategy of using motherhood, in fact, worked to deflect the critics and make feminism appeal to a wide range of women. Both these ends are necessary for a social movement to effect large changes in a culture. Of course, feminists have also supported motherhood because they wanted to give it its due. Millions of women find joy in motherhood, and millions of women will continue to mother no matter what other opportunities or choices are offered to them. The problem, though, has never been whether feminists should support motherhood, but rather, whether they should support motherhood *and* childlessness at the same time as equally acceptable but optional life-styles. Unfortunately, the two have often been viewed as incompatible.

Then, too, the women's movement has the same problem with childlessness as a social issue that other reform groups have with similar issues, namely, that it is and will remain the choice of a relatively small minority. Because of this, some feminists question how much an umbrella group can actually afford to sacrifice to defend the views of so few. Yet, the failure of the women's movement to support what amounts to genuine reproductive choice harms individuals as well as the movement.

Women who have already decided to have no children are not, as might be expected, the ones who most need the support of the women's movement. They have usually formed their own support systems among friends and acquaintances who are sympathetic to their decision. The tendency of these voluntarily childless women and childless couples to turn away from friends with children, as well as from persons who do not approve of their decision, and to reorient their lives around people who are like themselves has already been commented on. Because the direction of these people's lives is already set, they usually have few problems with their decision. But the millions of young women in their twenties and early thirties who are struggling with their ambivalence, who exist in a kind of limbo, could use the help of the women's movement. It could provide them with a support system in which to test their feelings, and it could also provide them with a much needed information network.

Providing this kind of support seems to be a job that is uniquely suited to the women's movement. A twenty-three-year-old woman touched on this need: "I know part of the reason I can't decide whether to have children is that I don't know enough about either motherhood or childlessness. For one thing, I would like to talk to other women who are considering childlessness. I would like to find out how they feel. I guess I would just like to see what they are like."

A forty-one-year-old childless woman who also felt an acute need to be connected with feminism on the issue of childlessness said, "I'm looking for a sense of continuity. I know that some women throughout history must have chosen childlessness. It can't be something that women suddenly decided to do ten years ago. There have to have been some precedents. Besides, look at how preoccupied women have been even since prehistorical times with birth control and with limiting childbearing. It must have been even more urgent to remain childless if there was a great risk that you might die in childbirth. That alone must have made many women yearn for childlessness. I think that much of women's history has been written by people in the women's movement, and I would like to see them devote more time to studying childless women and to the social implications of childlessness for women."

The First Wave of Feminism and Childlessness

To further understand why feminism has not been quicker to respond to childless and ambivalent women, it is necessary to backtrack into the nineteenth century and the first wave of feminism.

The first wave of feminists, most of whom were suffragists, were interested in controlling their own reproductive function, but they embraced motherhood as a means of doing so. Their stand on controlling reproduction was derived from the attitudes of the Victorian era from which this feminist movement emerged in the early nineteenth century and most particularly, from the Victorian views on the differences between the sexes. Suffragists argued that they deserved the right to vote (that was, in fact, their primary goal), the right to own property, and the right to control their own fertility *because* they were mothers. In the process of winning these rights, they deified motherhood not merely by historical accident but by design. The deification was the key element in a battle plan that inevitably backfired, for the day came when all that women were expected to do was mother, but it made good sense at the time.

Suffragists promoted motherhood for two reasons. The first was that, like good politicians anywhere, they saw that it was motherhood that made women unique. It was their trump card. A refusal to mother was what their male opponents feared most, so women's reassurances that their desire for greater freedom via suffrage not only would not interfere with motherhood but would, in fact, enhance it, was an astute political gesture.

As early as 1870, feminist Elizabeth Cady Stanton produced the kind of rhetoric that warmed the hearts of energetic reformers and calmed their fearful opponents. She said that "when a mother can give the world one noble, healthy man or woman, a perpetual blessing in the church and state, she will do better for humanity than in adding numbers alone, but with little regard to quality."[1] According to Stanton, any woman could reproduce and reproduction was essentially an animalistic act, but mothering—ah, there was the gift to mankind.

Another early feminist, Beatrice Hale, wrote in 1914: "The Age of Feminism is also the age of the child. The qualms of the timorous should be allayed by this fact, which proves that women, in gaining humanity, do not lose in womanliness."[2]

Thanks to early feminists, support of motherhood reached a state so close to godliness that in 1917 Anna May Wood, president of the Washington, D.C., Federation of Women's Clubs, a group that was decidedly nonfeminist, nevertheless took up the feminist strategy, announcing: "Motherhood glorifies women . . . any teaching that would tend to take from each woman the desire for motherhood is not ennobling to the race."[3]

The other reason that women jumped on the bandwagon to glorify motherhood was that they had no choice. Mothers were financially dependent upon men and had been since the Industrial

Revolution, when work moved from the home to the factory, thereby putting the balance of wage-earning power in the hands of those who worked outside the home, i.e., men. Motherhood gave women an important emotional hold over men, too. A woman with a child has always been harder to cast aside than a childless woman. One suspects that even prehistoric women were aware of their special status as mothers and used this knowledge to their advantage when organizing the first families. Certainly, until women had obtained economic control over their lives, they could not afford to alienate men by refusing to have children or by refusing to care for them. As a result, feminists' best strategy was to glorify motherhood, to consider it a source of strength, and to let it serve as a reminder of what women were owed.

Of course, women also embraced motherhood because, physically, they could do little to prevent it. In the nineteenth and early twentieth centuries, birth control was largely unavailable, illegal, and certainly unreliable. Because of the obvious, if not always fully understood, connection between bearing large numbers of children and having to endure a lifetime of fragile health or early death, however, women have long sought to control the number of children they bore. (Records show that prehistoric women and women in every civilization since early Greece and Rome have occupied themselves to some extent with methods of contraception.[4]) The reaffirmation of this connection by modern science led the early feminists to support birth control and to initiate what came to be called the "birth control movement."

But even though the first feminists supported birth control, they opposed contraception. They made a distinction between the so-called natural methods of birth control, such as withdrawal and abstinence, and what were viewed as unnatural, or contraceptive, methods, such as the use of condoms, diaphragms, and other similar devices. What differentiated the two was not that the latter involved the use of apparatuses while the former relied on willpower, but rather, the fact that one enabled women to control childbearing, while the other was used to perpetuate what were then viewed as men's natural and uncontrollably promiscuous natures. Early feminists' views about birth control and contraception stemmed from the Victorian definitions of masculinity and femininity. A man's sexual drive, the Victorians thought, required regular satisfaction through sexual intercourse, whereas a woman's sexual drive was satisfied through motherhood. In other words, men were sexual beings; women were maternal beings.

Social historian Linda Gordon, the author of an excellent book on the history of the birth control movement entitled *Woman's Body, Woman's Right,* took note of how this division strengthened the value of the maternal instinct:

> . . . that women might have the capacity for being sexual objects rather than mere objects, feeling impulses of their own, automatically tended to weaken the theory of the maternal instinct. In the fearful imagination of the self-appointed protectors of the family and of womanly innocence, the possibility that women might desire sexual contact not for the sake of pregnancy—that they might even desire it at the time when they did not want pregnancy—was a wedge in the door to denying that women had any special maternal instinct at all.[5]

Out of the birth control movement came something called the "voluntary motherhood movement," which emerged in the 1870s. The voluntary motherhood movement, composed as it was of such diverse groups as moral reformers, suffragists, and free lovers, was born out of women's desire to escape the tyranny of sexual relations they did not always welcome as well as unwanted and frequently life-threatening pregnancies.

Supporters of voluntary motherhood were united in believing that women owned and therefore should control their own bodies, that women's sexual drive was not substantially different from that of men, and that women should choose when to bear children. Opposed to contraception and abortion, they were nevertheless often sympathetic to women who had to have abortions. Supporters of voluntary motherhood advocated sexual abstinence as the preferred method of birth control. Contraception, they thought, would encourage promiscuity among men, and promiscuity often led to venereal disease. Since husbands often infected their wives with venereal disease, the possibility of contracting it was a legitimate fear of these women.

Moral reformers largely concerned themselves with these and other issues related to the sexual mores of the time. Suffragists wanted to expand women's roles as mothers and simultaneously to open up the professions to them. They also wanted to rearrange the social system so that women who had to work (no woman in that time, it was widely believed, *wanted* to work) would have a support system. Free lovers, although they were to remain a fringe group and therefore less influential in the voluntary motherhood movement than the other two groups, were also pro-motherhood. They simply wanted it separated from legal and/or religious marriage. All factions in the voluntary motherhood movement bolstered their case by saying that if women had fewer children, they would be able to devote more time to each child; thus would the overall quality of mothering be improved.

Early Roots of Childlessness

The voluntary motherhood movement provided the initial impetus for a consideration of childlessness as an option of true reproductive freedom for women.° Support for childlessness as a possible option was its logical extension. If women controlled their bodies, there was a possibility that some women would choose to exercise that control by not having children. Linda Gordon, agreeing with many other feminist historians, observed that many of these early "feminists and elite women—that is, still a relatively small group—were choosing not to marry or become mothers. That was primarily because of their increasing interest in professional work, and the difficulty of doing such work as a wife and mother."[6]

Despite what can now be seen as an essentially conservative ideology, the first wave of feminists—voluntary motherhood advocates, especially—drew criticism from even more conservative groups. The birth control movement was soon viewed as a female challenge to traditional male power, as well as a challenge to the family and to society.

All factions within the voluntary motherhood movement were quick to assure everyone else that they had no intention of destroying family life by not having babies. But in 1897 the National Congress of Mothers formed in reaction to voluntary motherhood

° Ironically, it was also the beginning of an extreme child-centeredness that culminated in the 1950s with what many view as excessive mothering, which, in turn, led to the rebellion in the 1960s of millions of women against the "feminine mystique."

supporters; it was an antifeminist group devoted, ironically, to defending motherhood against feminists who were themselves already defending it. In response, feminists elevated motherhood still higher.

A few radical feminists protested, but even they sought ways to accommodate both work outside the home and motherhood. No one was ready yet to openly suggest childlessness. Charlotte Perkins Gilman, in her economic treatises, discussed ways that domestic life might be better organized to make women's dual roles easier to handle, but never suggested that men, for example, might take on some of the domestic burdens. Instead feminists focused their efforts on winning the right to take on work outside their domestic sphere of activity while maintaining their responsibilities as wives and mothers. Women's willingness to take on more work rather than asking for some form of support from society or expecting their husbands to become true partners in their domestic lives has persisted until the present.

Not until the beginning of the twentieth century, over fifty years after the first wave of the women's movement, did some women begin to question whether the family—and along with it motherhood—had perhaps been too romanticized. One idea, however, had become crystal clear to a few early feminists: if their lives were to change for the better and if they were to pursue serious careers, they would have to consider having fewer, and in some cases, a few radicals allowed, no children. Thus, Elizabeth Cady Stanton toured the Midwest from 1869 to 1873 encouraging women to limit their childbearing.

Another feminist writer in the post-Civil War era, Eliza B. Duffey, wrote a book entitled *The Relations of the Sexes,* in which she stated that women did not need to have children unless they wanted them. She reassured women that no evil would befall them for not reproducing.[7] Duffey was among the first to recognize that an unwanted child suffered almost as much as its unwilling mother did. She wrote: "An unwilling motherhood is a terrible, a cruel, and unjust thing. . . . It embitters their lives and turns into a curse that which was meant to be a blessing."[8] But while Duffey in theory defended the right of a woman to remain childless if she so chose, her real intention was not to advocate childlessness so much as it was to encourage birth control. Of women who chose child-lessness, Duffey said, somewhat defensively, "Then don't let them have any. Their very lack of desire proves their unfitness."[9] That was about as far as childlessness had gotten as a feminist issue when the race-suicide war flared up.

The Race-Suicide War

As feminists were inching their way toward a discussion of child-lessness as one more option in genuine reproductive freedom, the backlash against the birth control movement gained strength. After several decades of lamenting the decline in the birth rate—that is, the decline among white, middle-class women compared to the ris-ing numbers of immigrants—many members of the establishment began to descry what they called "race suicide." It was an expres-sion that had been used for several decades, and it now became the rallying cry of a heated social and political debate.

Basically, the race-suicide war was an appeal to those who, in re-action to the voluntary motherhood movement, were afraid of what would happen if the "best" women stopped having babies or even if they had fewer babies than their mothers bore. (Even today, the same issue is occasionally raised, although *sotto voce* and in more acceptable language than the hysterical, racist rhetoric of the race-suicide war.) According to adherents of the race-suicide theory, any woman who did not willingly mother was shirking her duty and was, furthermore, selfish and coldhearted, epithets that have been used even today in some circles when the subject of childless women comes up.

Using metaphors he was comfortable with, President Theodore Roosevelt equated avoidance of motherhood with avoidance of mil-itary duty. Charges of race suicide were also used to condemn edu-cation for women as well as women who worked outside the home, since both groups were statistically less likely to marry and had fewer babies, when they did, than the general population. As the hysteria mounted, feminists, who were accused of devoting their energies to winning new status for women when they might better have been home making babies, became the scapegoats.

Gordon, who has written cogently and at length about the race-suicide war, described the chilling effect it had on women:

Roosevelt's attacks reverberated in widespread popular recognition of new values and practices and stimulated a wave of criticism against feminists, spinsters, childless women, and even mothers of small children. The hysteria lasted many years.[10]

Feminist response only showed the effectiveness of the attack. Some feminists agreed with supporters of race suicide that women had indeed been on the wrong track and should return to more traditional, home-oriented values; others shifted their ideology to place the blame on the economy and on society itself; and some brave women held their own and continued in the belief that women should have the right to control their reproductive destinies even if the result was greater tolerance of childless women. Among these women were two, a young woman who chose to remain anonymous and a prominent feminist, Ida Husted Harper. Both eloquently defended a woman's right to choose childlessness.

One of these defenses was a response to a speech Roosevelt delivered in 1905 to the National Congress of Mothers, in which he articulated his race-suicide views. Shortly afterward, *The Independent*, a weekly journal, printed an unsigned article entitled "Why I Have No Family." The document is as extraordinary as it is rare. (Linda Gordon, in researching her book, was unable to find a single signed article from the period defending childlessness.) It is extraordinary because the arguments put forth could as easily have been made in 1984 as in 1905. It is also extraordinary as a feminist document. The author, a young married editor and social reformer and a regular contributor to the journal under her own name, gave reasons for childlessness that are strikingly similar to the reasons that women give today:

> I never had any objections to motherhood; indeed, I had always been extremely fond of children. . . . [Children would] take most, if not all, of my time, and destroy my earning power and my social usefulness. My husband would have to more than double his income . . . and put all his energies into money-making, to the exclusion of his social work.[11]

Speaking of the joint decision she and her husband had made, she addressed herself to the charge that the decision to remain childless was selfish:

We are not selfish and pleasure loving; on the contrary, the
principal aim of our lives, as well as our standard of human
value, is social usefulness. Nor are we lonely and full of heart-
longings, as childless people are supposed to be. . . . We believe that to have children would be detrimental to our
usefulness as members of society, detract from the happiness
of our marriage, and make us lower, not nobler, people.[12]

The article also expressed the author's concern for women who
were solely dependent upon their husbands for support:

I have often reflected upon the position of the dependent wife
with a family. I had discovered that . . . there were num-
berless women in a state of hateful and hated marital servi-
tude. Whenever I learned of the reason of the women's
submission, it was always based upon the fact that she had
children and no money, the existence of the one precluding the
obtaining of the other.[13]

Another response to race-suicide charges had come earlier from
suffragist Harper, who wrote a signed article that stated what
many women had begun to think and feel, namely, that some
women and some couples were indeed happier and better off without children. Describing couples who married because they shared
many interests and who then found themselves driven apart by
their children, Harper used several examples to illustrate her point.
She also mentioned the expense of children, as well as the dangers
of childbirth, which were so great at the time her article appeared
that many women were unable to obtain life insurance. She
wrote:

Putting aside, however, the danger, the suffering, and all the
immediate inconveniences, think what it means for a woman to
give the core of her life, the beautiful years between twenty
and forty-five, the time when the mental powers are at
their best, when enjoyment in the pleasant things of the world
is keenest, to the exacting demands of the nursery. . . . It
would drive a man insane. . . . There never was a mother of a
large family who was willing that her daughters should have a
similar experience. . . . Conscientious women do not base
their expectations on the ground that "they can be something

better than the mother of children," but rather on their right to claim a part of life for what Elizabeth Cady Stanton so aptly calls the "Solitude of Self." For the public to insist that every marriage shall result in children is an impertinent interference with private rights. . . . There are innumerable ways of benefiting the world besides bringing a child into it.[14]

Although both the author of the anonymous article and Harper were mostly making a plea that childless women be granted a kind of "conscientious objector" status, even this view reflected a change in attitude. For what it did was to mark the beginning of recognition for childless women. Progress had been slow and would continue to be. Although cries of race suicide would fade away, women's struggle for reproductive freedom would be ongoing until the present. Not until the mid-twentieth century did childlessness really come off the unmentionable list for women. Even then, it was mostly among individual women rather than organized feminists that the subject was discussed.

After American women were granted suffrage in 1920, they more or less ceased their protests, naïvely believing that they had, in fact, achieved equality through the power of the ballot. The women's movement thus entered a dormant stage that was to last for more than forty years.

The Second Women's Movement and Childlessness

The women's movement renewed itself rather spontaneously in the 1960s, when women realized that the gains made during the struggle to win suffrage were neither so far-reaching nor so lasting as they had expected. Women had faltered in the workplace, earning less than men and still mostly toiling at "traditional" women's jobs. In academia, they had actually fallen behind previous levels, and a lower percentage of women earned graduate degrees in the 1960s than in the 1920s. In addition, a growing number of women were becoming frustrated with their rarefied lives as full-time mothers. Throughout the 1950s women had devoted themselves to their homes and children in a way that no preceding generation of women had ever before done. In an age when housework required an average of four hours per day, more middle-class women than ever before reported their full-time occupations as "housewife." Motherhood also had been expanded into a full-time occupation, and during this unique period, women of the rapidly growing middle class focused their daily lives around children and charity. The fact that a woman was supported by her husband was seen as a symbol of the family's upward mobility.

But signs of change were in the air. The bellwether of the second women's movement was a book called *The Feminine Mystique*, written in 1963 by Betty Friedan.[15] More radical theories would soon emanate from feminist pens, but *The Feminine Mystique* struck a nerve as no other publication did. It became the manifesto of a new wave of feminism that encompassed a wide range of women and which continues even today.

Once again in the 1960s, the role of motherhood in a woman's life was an issue with the feminists, but this time, there was no question of deifying it. This time the issues were of a more practical nature. The focus still was on motherhood to the exclusion of reproductive freedom and its concomitant right to choose childlessness. As with the first wave of feminism, women were divided over how motherhood could best be used to further their cause. The theme was essentially the same, but some of the approaches were new.

A special issue that mattered to many women—to those who considered themselves liberated and to those who lived more traditional lives—was how to place a value on women's services within the family, most specifically, on their services as mothers. Women had come to believe that by placing a monetary value on their services, they would gain the respect they clamored for. But by focusing so much attention on motherhood, women were in fact acquiescing to the idea that it remained their primary role. This inevitably led to an odd kind of expansion of the mother's role.

The new feminists were entering the workplace in unprecedented numbers, but they also breast-fed their children in unprecedented numbers. They became dedicated pronatalists, determined to prove that they could handle a career and motherhood. In a sense, they were promising that if they were allowed to expand on their role in the outside world, they would not do so at the expense of their role as mothers.

Women even seemed to be apologizing for their need to have fulfilling work outside the home. Instead of broadening their sphere of interests, though, they actually had shifted the focus of their lives to two major roles, where before the focus had been on one. Where women had previously devoted themselves to motherhood, they now just as conscientiously devoted themselves to motherhood *and* career, leaving themselves little time in between for anything else.

One woman who in her own words "capitulated" and had a child at age thirty-seven when she thought her career could tolerate it, said her life was a hectic round of activity that she could not tolerate for many more years: "There is an impossible amount of work to do, both in my career and for my family. When I'm not at work, my life is entirely centered on my child and my husband. Mostly on my child, though. I haven't gone anywhere alone with my husband in two years. I haven't read a serious book in that long. I feel so guilty that I'm not home all the time that I try to spend every waking minute when I'm not at work with my child. And sometimes, I really hate it that I have to drop my work and go home. There's lots of pressure that way, too. I don't like this, but I think it is the price I have to pay for having a career and being a mother. And it will only last a few more years, until my child is old enough to go places by himself and have his own friends."

In response to such pressures, feminists demanded support services that would accommodate working mothers. They wanted child-care facilities where women worked, flexible working hours, longer maternity leave, and no penalties for working less than full time.

Mostly such requests were ignored by those who had the power to change things, but they also created strife among feminists. An antinatalist faction formed; its members denigrated the work of housewives and mothers and generally held that women should refrain from having children in a world that gave so little support to do so. If women really wanted to make economic and professional strides, they argued, then they should do it on the (male) establishment's terms.

It was an in-group pronatalist-antinatalist fight from the beginning. Vast numbers of middle-class, traditional working women who might have subscribed to this new feminism had it offered them some relief could find nothing to help them in either side's arguments. Talk of changing the workplace to accommodate mothers scared women who did not yet need or want to work, and talk of refusing to have babies scared women—often already mothers—who were dependent on their husbands for support while they reared children. Once again, the women's movement was unable to address itself to childlessness—that would have paralyzed everyone.

But childlessness, the issue nobody wanted to deal with, was nonetheless rattling around in many women's minds. Ten years into the second wave of feminism, many women had discovered the pleasures of working, and an entire generation of young women who took it for granted that they would lead busy, exciting lives was entering the work force. Whether feminism was responsible or not, these women began to consider not when but *whether* they would have children.

How feminists stand on the issue of childlessness depends on how the current spate of childless women is interpreted. Are childless women a sign that all is not well within the social structure of society, most notably within the family? Is a more complete overhaul of the family necessary, as some have suggested, if women are to gain true equality? Or are childless women merely individuals whose numbers only make them appear to be a social trend or movement? Historian William L. O'Neill in his book *Everyone Was Brave: A History of Feminism in America* might think that childless women are symbolic of the former view, for as he has noted, there is some work left undone from the first feminist movement:

> By justifying their activities on the grounds that society was an extension of the home and woman's work in it merely an enlargement of her maternal powers, social feminists froze the domestic status quo. In effect they declared that it was not marriage and the family that needed to be changed, only certain social malformations that were inconsistent with the domestic ideal. Yet because it was the obligations imposed on women by their marital and familial roles that prevented them from achieving full equality, social feminism was far more social than feministic.[16]

In this wave of feminist struggles, as O'Neill suggests, if anything is to change, the emphasis must be on restructuring family life. And it must be restructured to accommodate women who are mothers and who need, for emotional or economic reasons, to work outside the home. Ultimately, it may not matter whether women who choose childlessness are viewed as individuals or as a social movement. Their message to feminists will be the same: there is more work to be done.

8.
WHAT MAKES WOMEN MOTHER?

When the question "What makes women mother?" is asked, the simplest, most basic, and until recently, the most frequently heard answer was: women mother because they have an innate drive—a maternal instinct—to do so. On the surface, it seems a simple enough answer to a fairly simple question. But upon examination, it becomes more obvious that the many possible layers of meaning inherent in this seemingly simple question make it about as easy to answer as the question "Why did you open that box, Pandora?" What is a "maternal instinct"? What actions or behaviors define it? Perhaps more important, especially to the 29 million women in their twenties and thirties who are contemplating childlessness, what does it mean to be with or without a maternal instinct, and can it be spoken of as something that one is either lacking or not lacking?

Absolute proof of the existence of a universal maternal instinct would jeopardize the entire notion that women are able and free to choose childlessness. If there were a maternal instinct, then wouldn't logic dictate that motherhood, rather than anything else, would be a woman's—all women's—life work? Wouldn't women become mothers despite any social, emotional, or intellectual forces beckoning them in other directions? In fact, wouldn't nature —Mother Nature?—resolve any small, leftover bits of ambivalence women might feel by making motherhood virtually irresistible to them? And for the occasional errant woman who did manage to escape the pull of motherhood and follow her own muse, couldn't one assume that there would be a price to pay, perhaps in terms of emotional or even physical well-being? Eventually, of course, we can turn all these questions around and ask how it is that so many women today are experiencing such profound maternal ambivalence—and why so many women are choosing childlessness—if the driving force behind the desire to mother is instinctual.

So many persons—experts and laypersons alike—have claimed that women mother because, in some way, they are instinctively driven to do so that it is only through an understanding of the arguments in support of a maternal instinct that the *idea* of a maternal instinct can be given personal definition by an individual woman—and dispelled if that is what is desired.

Generally speaking, the arguments on which a belief in a universal maternal instinct are based fall into three broad categories, which can be loosely defined as the biological, the psychological, and the cultural.

Adherents to the first general category believe that women mother because they have a biological urge to do so. Since the onset of the women's movement in the 1960s, which opened the door to deeper examination of women's roles than had been done for some time, feminists and many other women have regarded the notion that women might be biologically compelled to mother as a rather outdated concept. But recent developments in biological research have put many scientists to work on the renewed possibility that an instinct to nurture might be biologically based, after all. As we shall see, though, most of the research has been inconclusive, and some research work, most notably that done by John Money at Johns Hopkins, seems to disprove the idea that genetic or hormonal predilection can be used to fully explain nurturing behavior.

Others, mostly Freudians to one degree or another, adhere to the concept developed at the turn of the century that women mother because they are psychologically compelled to do so. The desire to mother is seen as one sign of being normal psychologically.

Finally, there are those experts—largely anthropologists, non-Freudian psychotherapists, and sociologists—who believe the primary reason women mother is because they are subjected to cultural pressure to do so.

There are several reasons to examine why women choose to mother. For some women, careful examination of the more concrete aspects of motherhood, such as how children can change a marriage or a career or the costs of rearing and educating children, helps to resolve the ambivalence. One woman, for example, was surprised to discover that her reservations about motherhood were based on a largely unfounded, in her case at least, fear that the responsibilities of parenting would fall almost entirely on her shoulders and that she could expect little help, let alone coparenting, from her husband. She commented, "Once I realized that my husband intended to be a full partner in parenthood, and that he had a great sensitivity toward my fears about motherhood, the issue was settled. I was free to acknowledge that I wanted a child."

For other women, more deeply mired in maternal ambivalence, the solution does not reside in an examination of the concrete aspects of motherhood, but rather it involves a more soul-searching, theoretical search that is concerned with the social and cultural implications of the decision to remain childless. The tangible shape of a woman's life as a voluntarily childless person largely has been the subject of this book thus far; in the following chapters, I shall deal with the more intangible, theoretical implications of the decision to remain childless.

The Public Image of Childless Women: Will It Change?

The desire to understand childlessness on a theoretical level also forces many women to confront something they would probably rather avoid: the image, which persists even today, of childless women as social deviants or rebels. This image is something that every childless woman must cope with occasionally. The extent to which any individual woman encounters this prejudice will depend upon her class, education, ethnic background, and her self-image, as well as her ability to ward off and ignore unwanted criticism of herself. In a sense, the "image problem" of childless women may perhaps be the ultimate form of pronatalist pressure, serving as it does to ostracize those who "dare" to choose childlessness and to warn those contemplating it of what lies ahead for them.

Society chooses to view childlessness as a radical action. Unlike other forms of radicalism, though, which are often self-selected, labels such as "socially aberrant" or "deviant," or even "abnormal," are not welcome appellations—nor are they accurate descriptions of those who choose childlessness. In fact, childless women do not consider themselves radical or deviant, nor do studies or conversations with childless women show them to be anything other than well-adjusted, feminine women who mostly adhere to traditional values.

Despite this, however, the image of childless women as social deviants persists. Which brings us to the question of why society insists on labeling a nonvocal, nonproselytizing minority in such provocative terms. The most obvious answer is fear, the fear that given any encouragement, any official sanction, still more women will choose childlessness. Men have probably always harbored a fear that women would not willingly bear children if there were not social pressure of some sort on them to do so. As for women, presented with an array of new role models, some of which might appear to preclude motherhood, they have begun to view childlessness as an exciting new option.

The answer also is based on a recognition of reality with respect to how cultures are organized. Despite the fact that childless women do not consider themselves radical or socially deviant, in one sense they are, simply by virtue of having chosen a life role that the overwhelming majority of women in our culture do not choose. Particularly in a culture such as ours, where females, until recently, have been taught from a young age that their primary role in life was to mother, childlessness must necessarily be viewed, to some extent, as a *reaction* to motherhood. Not to acknowledge this fact is to fail to comprehend some of the deepest implications of childlessness.

Acknowledging the reactionary element in the decision to remain childless, however, does not mean that childless women are radicals, at least in the way that this word is usually defined. In fact, this is a label that childless women have grounds to reject, for they have never organized for political purposes, nor have they attempted to make childlessness a *cause célèbre* in any way. As a group, childless women are surprisingly "normal." Most of the time, in fact, their only act of social deviancy is childlessness. In choosing it, however, childless women are social deviants in the sense that they have not opted for the norm, i.e., the life of the majority. It is in this sense, too, that childless women are so often labeled radical, socially deviant, or abnormal.

However much childless women might want to escape this sort of labeling and all that it implies, until the day when women are truly free to choose between motherhood and childlessness, and until the day when both roles are presented as viable, socially accepted options, childless women will have to cope with being outsiders in their own culture. Their best defense, for those times when one is needed, is to understand the forces that led most women to mother, so they can also fully understand their decisions not to mother.

Reproduction Versus Motherhood

As a preface to the discussion of the biological bases for a maternal instinct, it is necessary to clarify the difference between reproduction and motherhood. Because of the emotional content that surrounds the question of whether or not there is a biologically based maternal instinct, the two are often confused. For the record, reproduction is the clearly defined set of events, i.e., fertilization of the ovum by the sperm and gestation in the mother's womb, that culminate with the birth of a child. In other words, reproduction is over at the moment of birth. Normally, direct intercourse between a man and a woman is required for reproduction to occur.° The act of reproduction is entirely physical.

Motherhood, by contrast, consists of the twenty-odd years that follow reproduction and involves a physical and emotional commitment on a woman's part that she will, to the best of her ability, attend to the physical and emotional needs of her child. A good mother is someone with the capacity to nurture.

Searching for the Maternal Instinct

In order for a biological maternal instinct to exist in a scientific sense, it must be measurable. Because of this, biologists have attempted to find its source in women's genes and/or hormones.

Some interesting research on sexual development was conducted by psychologist John Money and a team of researchers at Johns

° In these days of genetic engineering, this is no longer true, but for purposes of comparison, it will be assumed that intercourse between a man and a woman is necessary for reproduction to occur.

Hopkins University, and much of this is applicable to whether or not an innate biological drive to nurture, in fact, does exist. Of particular interest was Money's work with two categories of hormonally and genetically aberrant persons, males with androgen-insensitivity syndrome and females with Turner's syndrome.[1]

The former are genetic males who cannot use the androgen their testicles produce. They are born with female genitalia. At birth, despite their male XY chromosomes, they are usually assigned to the female sex because of their appearances, and they are reared as females. These males typically exhibit the role behavior that would be expected of any female child in Western culture. They play with dolls; they wear and enjoy feminine clothes; and they assume feminine mannerisms. They share interests normally associated with girls and women, including a strong desire to become mothers. Some of these XY males have, in fact, married and adopted children. As mothers, they have proven to be every bit as nurturant as any genetic female. Yet these "mothers" are biological males. They lack complete female reproductive organs and have undescended testicles; they do not menstruate or ovulate; and there is neither a genetic nor a hormonal basis for their desire—and proven ability—to mother.

A complementary example is provided by XO females, who have Turner's syndrome. Because of a genetic mishap, an XO female is born without ovaries. She is lacking the XX chromosome combination that would make her a genetically normal female. XO infants are reared as females even though they are incapable of giving birth and do not produce estrogen or other female sex-linked hormones. In other words, XO females have neither the genes nor the hormones of normal females. Since they are not biologically programmed to mother, one would expect these women, or at least a higher number than might be found in the normal female population, to show little interest in mothering. Yet research shows that XO females have as many fantasies about children and their capacities to nurture them as do normal girls. XO females also have made excellent adoptive mothers.

These two examples would seem to indicate that there is no basis for believing that desire to nurture is motivated by genes. Apart from these two examples, scientists' attention has also turned to the role that hormones might play in proving or disproving the existence of a maternal instinct.

The role played by sex hormones in humans was discovered during the first two decades of the 1900s, when scientists began to understand that these substances, produced by the body's endocrine glands and circulated throughout the bloodstream to all parts of the body, possibly were the long-sought-after link between the mind and the body. The presence of hormones, scientists thought, for the most part correctly, would explain many things about human behavior. Because two important functions of sex hormones were to precipitate puberty and to maintain postpubertal, i.e., adult, sexual functions, they were soon touted as the regulators of most sex-linked behavior in men and women. The male hormones androsterone and testosterone were thought to be what made men "masculine," and the female hormones estrogen and progesterone were thought to be what made women "feminine."

It is not possible to consider the functions of hormones without also noting the influence of psychoanalysis, which was establishing its own definitions of masculinity and femininity at approximately the same time that conclusions were being drawn about the role of hormones in the human body. This exciting new science, the first in several hundred years significantly to expand medical knowledge about the human psyche, had an important influence on biological thinking. Partly because Freud himself was a physician, he chose to describe his discoveries about the human mind in biological terms. So important was the development of psychoanalysis in medical circles that for decades thereafter, research in certain areas, most notably human sexual research, was cast in psychoanalytic terms. Thus, the behavioral traits ascribed to hormonal activity were defined as being either masculine or feminine, and masculinity and femininity, in turn, were defined by the psychoanalysts. For example, the presence of the hormone estrogen was credited with making women nurturing; and nurturing was tagged as a feminine trait by the psychoanalysts. Thus, the ability to nurture came to be considered an innate female trait. The same line of reasoning was applied to testosterone as a source of men's innate ability to be aggressive. Eventually, these traits and many others in men and women came to be viewed as largely exclusive to one sex or the other, and often the traits were paired, albeit as polar opposites.

Thus, aggressiveness was seen to be an innate trait in men, while, at the opposite pole, the ability to nurture, or mother, was considered an innate trait of females.

Some researchers have attempted to make a connection between hormonal activity in biological mothers and the triggering of the desire to nurture. Recent research on the influence of hormones on the capacity to nurture is scarce and fairly inconclusive, but there are no definitive research results to suggest that nurturing is hormonally based. In one experiment, male and virgin female rats injected with estrogen did exhibit an increase in nurturing behavior.[2] But this can be interpreted at best as proof that estrogen predisposes one to nurture, and besides, there are other ways to induce nurturing behavior. In fact, in male rats, nurturing behavior has been triggered merely by exposing them to their young, although their nurturing behavior does tend to unlock slightly more slowly than in biological mothers.[3]

In comparisons between biological mothers and other females, the nonmothering (in animal species, usually virgin) females exhibited as much nurturing behavior and cared as well for the young as did biological mothers.[4] One contemporary British study of humans revealed that of 180 adopted children, most of them by age seven were doing well, and in many cases, better, than children reared with their biological mothers.[5]

Many researchers studying humans and animals have noted that "maternal," or nurturing, behavior can be stimulated in virgin females and in men by the presence of an infant. One study showed that both men and women react in similar ways to infant sounds of pain and pleasure. The measure used was the changes in pupil size, which are known to reflect affection in humans by growing larger.[6]

Furthermore, if female sex hormones can trigger nurturing behavior, then the opposite should also be true, namely, that male sex hormones would cut off or reduce nurturing behavior. Money and his associates were able to work with a number of females who had received an overdose of androgens prenatally. (Their mothers had been treated with androgens to prevent miscarriage; it was a common medical treatment during the 1940s before researchers discovered that this would masculinize the fetus.) These girls were born with masculinized genitalia, so their abnormality was obvious from birth.

Money did extensive studies to correlate the behavior of a control group of normal girls with the overandrogenized ones. In general, he found that the overandrogenized group tended to be tomboys, a fact that seemed to support the notion that hormones influence maternal behavior. Money reported that the girls preferred "the utilitarian and functional in clothing rather than the chic, pretty, or fashionably feminine"; they preferred careers over marriage; they fantasized less than the control group about marriage and children; and they were slower to start dating. The overandrogenized females tended to be less responsive to dolls than to other toys. Money also found, however, that they were no more aggressive than the control group, that there were no differences between the two groups in their childhood sexuality or preferences for sexual play, and that the overandrogenized girls did not reject marriage, but rather, stated a preference to combine it with a career. All the girls in the control group wanted to be mothers, whereas one third of the overandrogenized females said they preferred not to have children.[7]

A closer look at this research, done in the 1950s and reviewed in the light of social developments in the two subsequent decades, reveals that he and his researchers may have fallen into a trap, namely, that of using learned sex-role behaviors as proof of a biological predilection. For example, playing with dolls was viewed as a rehearsal for motherhood, and putting a career before marriage was viewed as unfeminine behavior. The selection of clothes that were "utilitarian and functional" rather than "chic, pretty, or fashionably feminine" was seen as a measure of femininity rather than as a nonsexist matter of taste.[8]

Nancy Chodorow, author of *The Reproduction of Mothering*, and several other researchers have challenged the Money research. Chodorow noted:

> In some of the childhood cases, sex was reassigned from boy to girl in infancy, or they had operations to create more feminized genitalia. In all cases, therefore, parents knew about their daughters' abnormalities. The evidence about them comes from self-report and mothers' reports. In some cases parents were explicitly warned not to discourage tomboyishness for fear of counterreaction on their daughters' part, and there is no

information provided on what the girls themselves knew or were told about themselves.[9]

Furthermore, the Money study did not follow up on the girls past the age of sixteen, so the adult lives of these women are unknown. Whether they forged successful careers, whether they ultimately rejected marriage in favor of careers, or whether they became successful adoptive mothers is not known.

The most startling finding in Money's research, however, is that one third of the overandrogenized females preferred to have no children and that many of these girls stated a preference to combine marriage with careers. The real interest these girls as a test group have for us may lie in the fact that they were reared without the extreme cultural pressure that most girl children experience. Because the overandrogenized girls' parents knew about their children's deformed genitals and did not know what lay ahead for their children, i.e., whether they would be able to lead lives as normal females, it is safe to say that these parents let up on the pressure on their children to lead traditional female lives. Certainly, research results suggest that the pressure on this group was considerably less than for the control group. This suggests that without the cultural pressure that is usually brought to bear on girls and women to conform, in part by putting marriage ahead of a career and babies ahead of everything else, a much higher proportion of women than has been previously supposed might grow up and choose to remain child-free.

Learning How—and How Not—to Mother

If there is, as yet, no real proof that maternal behavior is determined by genes or hormones, there is a growing body of evidence to suggest that nurturing is learned. It comes from animal studies and from studies of various human cultures.

Anthropological research, primarily that of Margaret Mead, has lent credence to the view that women do not mother naturally but must be taught to do so. It was in 1935 in the groundbreaking book *Sex and Temperament in Three Primitive Societies* that Mead offered the first, and now classic, examples of the great variety of styles of mothering, which, in turn, would seem to indicate that even what is taught about motherhood varies from culture to culture and has done so throughout history.[10] Although Mead observed three cultures, two suffice to illustrate that the ability to nurture most likely is not innate or even necessarily universal.

She wrote of a Papuan people called the Arapesh, an unusually gentle, nonaggressive mountain group on the island of New Guinea whose chief concerns in life were child rearing and farming. Both sexes were socialized similarly, and as a result both participated fully in parenthood, as Mead noted:

> The minute day-to-day care of little children, with its routine, its exasperations, its wails of misery that cannot be correctly interpreted, these are as congenial to the Arapesh men as they are to the Arapesh women.[11]

The father even undergoes a "lying-in" period at the same time that his wife gives birth, when both husband and wife fast and perform certain rituals designed to ensure the health and happiness of their newborn.

The Arapesh do not recognize that the father's role in conception is completed once intercourse takes place. They believe that frequent intercourse is needed during the early stages of pregnancy to shape and feed the fetus. However, when the mother begins to show visible signs of pregnancy, sexual intercourse becomes taboo in order to ensure that the mother will have a calm pregnancy. The taboo lasts until the child is old enough to walk, and even extends to the husband's other wife, if he has one. Its purpose is to protect the child and give it the undivided attention of its parents during its early months of life.

By contrast, another Papuan people, the Mundugumor, a river-dwelling, cannibalistic tribe whose relations between the sexes are characterized by hostility and anger, avoid pregnancy and dislike giving birth, the women as much as the men. Relations between a husband and wife break down as soon as they recognize that she is pregnant, and neither takes any joy in the pregnancy.

Where the Arapesh of both sexes are kind and gentle with their children, the Mundugumor are mean and even cruel. An Arapesh mother frequently has her child on her lap or nearby, and it claims her attention easily; it may sleep curled alongside her at night, and during the day she carries it with her in a soft, flexible pouch that is thin enough for the baby to feel the warmth of her body.

The Mundugumor mother resents her baby's demands and responds to them only with reluctance. The infant spends most of its time in a rigid, thick basket through which it cannot possibly feel the warmth of its mother's body; but then, its mother often leaves it alone, anyway, when she leaves the house for brief outings.

The Mundugumor infant is fed only after it has cried for a while. When it begins to cry, its mother or some other woman attempts to quiet it by making a harsh scratching noise against its basket. The mother often breast-feeds the infant standing up, hurriedly, and she lashes out in anger at the infant if it chokes or burps. The Arapesh mother, by contrast, feeds her infant on demand and draws out mealtime by talking and playing games with the baby.

The sharply contrasting styles of motherhood of the Arapesh and Mundugumor—and anthropological files are filled with many more examples and variations—tend to point toward the conclusion that maternal behavior is largely the result of cultural learning. Zoologists have long suspected that this is true. They have observed that most animals do not even know how to care for their young unless they are taught to do so—usually by living at their mother's side for an extended period of time.

In one study that measured the mothering skills of Japanese monkeys, the degree of a mother's skill was found to be dependent upon her having had previous experience in communal child rearing. Some new mothers were utterly inept: they stepped on their infants, were incapable of nursing them, and left them in the sun, which nearly killed them.[12]

Another study rated maternal behavior among captive chimpanzees and found that it ranged from incompetent to neglectful to abusive. The chimpanzees were rated on their mothering skills on a scale of 1 to 5. Of nineteen chimps who had lived with their mothers fewer than eighteen months, only one received a rating of 5, and six of the ten who were reared with their mothers for more than eighteen months received a 1 rating.[13]

In another study, laboratory-raised rhesus monkeys were found to know little even about giving birth, something that many scientists have assumed was instinctive even if the ability to nurture was learned. The rhesus monkeys did not know how to dispose of the placenta or the umbilical cord and in some cases, could not even tell the two apart. They had no idea how to care for their infants immediately after birth.[14]

Even breast-feeding appears to be a learned skill. In one study of female chimpanzees, again reared away from their mothers, some were found to make stabs at nursing but to be unable to feed regularly or efficiently enough to ensure the survival of their infants. The chimps did not reflexively or instinctively place the infants at their breasts, nor did they attempt to carry their infants near their breasts. In other studies cited in the same source, among several other species of animals, first-time mothers were less competent at nursing than were mothers who had given birth several times.[15]

In research on humans, Ann Oakley, in her book *Sex, Gender and Society,* cited a study of 150 human mothers who did not know how to breast-feed, but, rather, had to be taught how to do this.[16] The existence of the La Leche League and other support groups to help mothers learn how to nurse their infants, and the fact that breast-feeding comes and goes almost as a matter of fashion (with no ill effects on the mothers who do not nurse), support the notion that there is nothing natural or innate about a mother's ability to nurse, other than her ability to produce milk. Some scientists have even questioned the belief that only a natural mother can nurse, and there are occasional random reports of adoptive mothers who have managed to produce milk for their babies.

Apart from the factual evidence introduced by these examples suggesting that mothering behavior is learned and not instinctive, several questions of a more philosophical nature present themselves. For instance, if a maternal instinct exists, then why is it that all women do not mother? Researchers working in communities where birth control is not practiced for religious reasons, and where children are highly valued, have found that the average woman is capable of bearing about nine children.[17] Yet, in few cultures anywhere in the world have most women elected to have this many children. Since effective methods of birth control have come into existence, in fact, the birth rate has steadily declined. Furthermore, in almost all cultures since prehistoric times, a great deal of evidence exists to suggest that women have, with varying degrees of success, always attempted to control the number of births.[18] Economic depression temporarily causes the birth rate to decline, too, for no reason other than the fact that women elect to have fewer or no babies.

Then, too, if mothering is innate, how does one explain cruel or neglectful mothers? Mothers who abandon their children? How does one explain a culture such as that of Renaissance Europe in which the babies of rich women were routinely sent to wet nurses, even though two thirds of the infants sent very far away and one fourth of those sent to wet nurses who lived near the mother died?[19] How does one explain a culture such as that of eighteenth-century France, where the abandonment of newborn infants was so commonplace as to lead to the invention of a device called a *turret,* whose sole function was to facilitate the act of abandoning a child? Social historians attribute the increase of foundlings in one home from 312 children in 1740 to 131,000 in 1859 to the use of the *turret.*[20]

How does one explain mothers who murder their children? Or the fact that, almost universally and throughout history, it is mothers who have practiced infanticide?[21] Why are illegitimate children accepted more readily in some periods of history, most notably in affluent ones, than in other, leaner times? How can the maternal instincts of spinsters, young widows, and nuns be ignored? If mothering were instinctual, wouldn't these women be driven to mother regardless of any social consequences or ostracism they might suffer as a result?

To summarize, it appears that a maternal instinct, if indeed it exists at all, cannot be directly tied to any specific biological function. There is, on the contrary, a great deal of evidence to suggest that both humans and animals must learn the physical and nurturing skills required to mother successfully.

Despite the advances that are being made daily in biology, there may never be a definitive answer that settles once and for all whether mothering is biologically induced for the simple reason that it may always be impossible to separate the biological, or innate, function from what is culturally induced, as psychoanalyst Maria Piers has so astutely noted:

> I'm not happy with the distinction between inborn and cultural elements, because I've never seen anybody or any kind of

inborn propensity that could develop more than half an inch
without the cultural matrix. Furthermore, I have never met
anyone outside a human culture, and I think it would be impossible to establish beyond the shadow of a doubt whether
the maternal instinct is an inborn or a genetically present capacity to care for the young, weak and helpless, or whether it
is part of the gross process we call enculturation.[22]

By 1949, long before women were publicly announcing their intentions to remain childless or even weighing the possibility, Margaret Mead was mulling over childlessness and motherhood and
the possible motivations of each. She concluded:

Women, like men, are creatures who learn; their behavior as
adults is dependent upon their childhood experiences. They
can so learn not to want children that they become dangerous
to all life on earth.

But there seems to be no reliable evidence to suggest that
learning not to want children necessarily introduces such a
deep conflict into a woman's nature that the conflict is insolu-
ble and she must inevitably pay a price, in frustration or
hatred of her fate, that will in turn reverberate in the lives
around her.[23]

Unfortunately, for the fate of women over the past few decades,
Freud did not agree.

9.
SIGMUND FREUD AND THE MATERNAL INSTINCT

Sigmund Freud thought the urge to nurture was unique to women, and that it was, furthermore, part of any normal woman's psychological makeup. In Western culture, since the nineteenth century, the idea of a maternal instinct has largely been defined by the Freudian theory of psychosexual development. Other theories of human psychosexual development have been created, but none has carried the weight of Freudian thought, and many have merely been extensions of it. Freudian theory has largely been responsible for making motherhood what it has become in twentieth-century Western culture: a virtual psychological mandate. According to the Freudian definition of femininity, a normal woman was a woman who wanted to be a mother. Women who rejected motherhood were abnormal, meaning, in effect, neurotic or even psychotic.

Although other factors such as the Industrial Revolution and Victorian attitudes toward women and sex also played a role in shaping the way motherhood is viewed, at its core, today the psychological mandate to mother mostly consists of the thought of Sigmund Freud and his followers.

Freud Versus Feminism

Unfortunately, Freud's defenders have at times done him great damage, and that in turn has brought on what might without exaggeration be called the wrath of feminist theorists and writers. Any discussion of the Freudian influence on any aspect of women's lives must necessarily touch upon the clash between Freud's followers and feminists. Marxist-feminist historian Shulamith Firestone wrote that Freudian thought and feminism actually sprang from common roots in that both were reactions to the extreme sexual repression of the Victorian era. Feminists, however, sought to change the status quo, while Freud's followers attempted to explain it—with the result that they became its greatest defenders. This is not necessarily something that Freud himself would have approved, for he had expressed his doubts about whether he had correctly explained femininity:

> . . . the great question that has never been answered and which I have not been able to answer, despite my thirty years of research into the feminine soul, is "What does a woman want?"[1]

Feminist writers have been quick to call attention to how ineptly and inaccurately Freud's theories, especially with regard to femininity, have been interpreted. However antagonistic they have, at times, appeared to be toward Freudian thought, these writers have nonetheless served an important function by drawing attention to the abuses of Freud's thought and to the ways that it has come to be used as a social tool to keep rebellious, i.e., nonmothering, women in line. Too often, Freudian theory has been used to "cure" women of their "aberrant" urges by reshaping them for motherhood. This has been a disservice to Freud and certainly to the women who fell under the spell of this kind of thinking.

Despite the use to which Freudian thought has been put since Freud's death, its influence cannot be underestimated. It captured the imagination of experts and laypersons alike, and it shook the dust off Victorian thinking. Freudian theory influenced many schools of therapy for decades and continues to dominate some today. In particular, it shaped the way our culture views women, and it is this that influences our attitude toward childless women.

The power that psychoanalytic thought exerted over women's lives, however, was not without precedent. In fact, part of the reason that Freudian thinking took hold as it did must be attributed to the sway the medical establishment already held over women's lives. At the time Freud started to develop his theories, women had been convinced that they were fragile, inherently ill creatures who required careful handling and were deserving of special if not equal status by virtue of the fact that they were mothers. For a while, Freudian theory even looked like an advance in women's health:

> Under Freud's influence, the scalpel for the dissection of female nature eventually passed from the gynecologist to the psychiatrist. In some ways, psychoanalysis represented a sharp break with the past and a genuine advance for women: it was not physically injurious, and it did permit women to have feelings. . . . But in important ways, the Freudian theory of female nature was in direct continuity with the gynecological view which it replaced. It held that the female personality was inherently defective. . . . Women were still "sick," and their sickness was predestined by anatomy.[2]

A Theory of the Maternal Instinct: Freud's Psychosexual Model

To understand the Freudian definition of femininity is to understand why so few women have embraced childlessness or even acknowledged feelings of maternal ambivalence. Although Freud never labeled his work as such, his theory of feminine psychosexual development is nonetheless a portrait of the psychological maternal instinct. Unfortunately, like any other portrait, it turned out not to be reality so much as an image of what its creator thought reality looked like.

Freud was the first person to develop a model—or rather, a two-part model, one for men and one for women—to explain the psychosexual development of human beings. Underlying this theory were several earlier theories he had developed, namely, that all humans were subject to certain innate, universal drives, and that these drives motivated all human activity.

Freud's model of female psychosexual development was directly based on his version of male psychosexual development, a fact that has created some consternation among feminists, as well as among many scientists and researchers. A plea has often been made for someone to create a completely separate model of feminine development that is not based on a masculine model, but to date, no one has accomplished this. And even if such a model were drawn up, as it almost certainly will be, it would hardly eradicate the influence of Freudian thought, which is pervasive in Western culture.

In developing the female psychosexual model, based, as just noted, on the male model, Freud, for example, interpreted the female clitoris as being a vestige of the male penis. Such thinking, it must be acknowledged, was in keeping with the time in which Freud lived, for the most advanced biological research of that day held that, physically speaking at least, the female anatomy appeared to be a case of arrested development—something that had failed to turn into a male.

Freud postulated that a woman's long and fairly complicated path to developing a maternal instinct began when as a little girl she discovered that she did not have a penis. Thus began her oedipal journey, which, if all went well, would culminate with the replacement of the desire for a penis with a desire for a child. Freud wrote:

> When the little girl discovers her own deficiency, from seeing a male genital, it is only with hesitation and reluctance that she accepts the unwelcome knowledge. As we have seen, she clings obstinately to the expectation of one day having a genital of the same kind, too, and her wish for it survives long after her hope has expired. The child invariably regards castration in the first instance as a misfortune peculiar to herself; only later does she realize that it extends to certain other children and lastly to certain grown-ups. When she comes to understand the general nature of this characteristic, it follows that femaleness —and with it, of course, her mother—suffers a great depreciation in her eyes.[3]

Not only does a female child's mother suffer by comparison, but, as Freud noted, "After a woman has become aware of the wound to her narcissism, she develops, like a scar, a sense of inferiority." Until she makes this discovery, however, the "sexuality of a little girl is of a wholly masculine character."[4]

The problem for the little girl is how to reassign a sense of value to herself after her shocking discovery. Once the little girl has grasped her innate inferiority, she can, in fact, begin to redeem herself by transferring her erotic affection from her mother, who is now tarnished in her eyes anyway, to her father. At first, her attraction to him is based on the hope that he will be able to give her a penis. When she discovers that this is not to be, she channels her wish for a penis into a wish for a child, or at least she does that if she manages a healthy resolution of her oedipal crisis. Freud called these women "claimers." They became mothers.

But not every woman managed to be a claimer, so Freud devised two other categories to describe outcomes of the feminine oedipal crisis. For example, a woman might deny her sexuality or be unable to respond sexually, but still accept the innate power of men over women, that is, the idea that women's role is passive compared to the more active or dominant one of men. Such women Freud called "acceptives." Alternately, and even more disastrously, a woman could deny reality, reject men entirely, possibly even becoming masculine in her orientation. In extreme instances, her clitoris might become a substitute penis. Freud called these women "renouncers."

Claimers, of course, readily accepted motherhood since the desire to mother was the result, he said, of a healthy resolution to the oedipal crisis for a woman. Childless women and women who were ambivalent about motherhood tended to be either acceptives or renouncers, Freud said, although presumably, with enough of the right kind of prodding, acceptives could be cajoled or even coerced into motherhood. The plight of renouncers, however, was more ominous, as the French psychoanalyst Marie Bonaparte, an early disciple of Freud, noted:

The *renouncers*, finally, are women whom the discovery of the difference between the sexes has so disheartened, discouraged, and rebuffed that they prefer to abandon all use of their sexuality. Thus, biologically outclassed by the male, they abandon all sexual rivalry with him. The totally frigid, who nevertheless have accepted the male, belong to the class of acceptives, though inhibited for the time being. The true renouncers truly abandon risking the male's embrace and try not to compete with him in his own domain. Mostly, they provide the armies of spinsters given to feminine social functions: mother substitutes, nurses, nursemaids, school teachers, social workers, often desexualized more or less; they are a kind of human counterpart of the worker masses among ants and bees. They must be far rarer among primitives than with us, for the primitive woman cannot so easily evade her childbearing role.[5]

According to Bonaparte and other psychoanalysts, women were ill not only if they resisted motherhood but also if they competed in the workplace with men or otherwise sought careers for themselves. And if these women sought careers, they would naturally gravitate toward occupations where they could play out their frustrated maternal instincts, anyway.

The "Maternal" Orgasm

Not only did Freud postulate that normal women had to replace their longings for a penis with longings for a baby, but he outlined one more developmental task that was necessary before a woman could flower into mature femininity, i.e., into motherhood.

He had observed that a little girl's sexuality was centered on her clitoris, whereas the sexuality of an adult woman was centered on her vagina. On the basis of this observation, Freud theorized that a switch from the clitoris to the vagina as the source of female orgasm was a necessary step in the psychological growth of a woman. It was normal for little girls, whom Freud, after all, characterized as nothing other than "little men" prior to resolution of their oedipal crisis, to focus on their clitorises, because as he wrote: "We are justified in assuming that for many years the vagina is virtually non-existent and possibly does not produce sensations until puberty."[6] By the time she became an adult, however, a woman was supposed to have focused on her vagina as a center for sexual feelings. That was, to Freud's way of thinking, the only normal source of orgasmic sensation in a mature woman. Only an immature woman, the kind of woman who might resist the notion that her primary source of psychological fulfillment lay in motherhood, he said, would continue to derive sexual satisfaction from clitoral orgasm.

Bonaparte even saw a connection between the kind of orgasm a woman experienced and her desire to mother:

> The wish for maternity—I do not say the more or less enforced acceptance of the child—is a factor so favorable to vaginalization that at times, one is surprised to learn that highly domes-

tic women are often the best adapted to their erotic function. Nothing wounds the narcissism of clitoridal women more, given their sense of resentment, than discovering this. Generally, however, they do not believe it.

Physical inacceptance of the maternal function and defective maternal instinct, however, also seems no less frequently related to the normal failure in women to establish the erotic function [the switch, that is, from clitoral to vaginal feeling]. . . . Similarly pathogenic to the erotic feminine function would appear to be the lack of identification with the mother, who remains overdetermined as the love object in the unconscious and, deriving therefrom, the absence of a true maternal instinct, leading to a psychical rejection of motherhood, of children to come.[7]

In a sense, Freudians had decided that women not only had to want children to be considered normal, but they had to prove they wanted them by switching their erotic focus from their clitorises to their vaginas.

Western culture was enraptured by the Freudian idea that women somehow were psychologically mandated to mother, and from there it was a short jump to the conclusion that all women should be mothers. Given the relatively widespread acceptance of Freudian thinking in the Western world, it is not surprising that few women were strong enough psychologically or intellectually to challenge Freud's theory of psychosexual development.

Another reason Freud's theory was not challenged, though, can be attributed to the fact that it was, in one sense, not new at all. Admittedly, some aspects of the theory were new, but the life experiences to which Freud applied them were not. Freud merely gave definition to what already existed. He described what women had been doing for centuries and motherhood as it had existed in patriarchal Western cultures for a long time. Motherhood had always been the primary vehicle through which a woman could obtain recognition.

Therefore, part of the appeal of Freudian thinking to women undoubtedly was that it felt right. Even a forward-thinking woman who might feel some dismay at getting the kind of confirmation Freudian theory seemed to provide probably would not have ever considered challenging Freud or his followers. The main reason, though, that women accepted Freudian ideas about themselves was touched upon earlier: given the lack of reliable contraception throughout most of history, women did not see themselves as having any choice other than motherhood. What Freud had really done for women, unfortunately, was to give motherhood psychological definition as a *rite de passage* that delivered a young girl quivering on the brink of womanhood into full-blown femininity.

In an atmosphere permeated by such thinking, it is hardly surprising to find that the childless woman was defined mostly in pejorative and negative terms. Women who were infertile suffered the somewhat dubious distinction of being at least considered innocent, if somewhat pitiable, victims of their plight. By contrast, the image of a woman who chose childlessness crystallized into that of a person who was aberrant, abnormal, rebellious, and certainly asocial—perhaps even a threat to her culture, as Mead suggested.

Reexamining Freud
in the Light of Scientific Discovery

Much of what Freud postulated about women and maternal feelings, especially his theories about the two kinds of orgasm and the maternal instinct, was eventually disproven by later scientific discoveries about the nature of human beings, and particularly, about the nature of their sexual lives. Freud may even have sensed that he was on the wrong track, or at least, he probably would have eagerly embraced more data about women's sexuality as a means of confirming or disproving his own speculations. In the following statement he seemed to be expressing his own misgivings about the nature of femininity: "If you want to know more about femininity, inquire from within your own experience, or turn to the poets, or wait until science can give you deeper more coherent information."[8]

About fifty years passed before science began to come up with some answers. It is now known, for example, that, if anything, it is men who are biologically descended from women, rather than the other way around. According to embryologists, fetuses begin life destined to be female, and only an internal injection of testosterone causes the fetus to differentiate into a male. It also becomes impossible, in the light of this research, to accept the clitoris as an inferior penis.

Pioneer sex researchers William Masters and Virginia Johnson also put to rest the notion that women experience two totally different kinds of orgasm, one of which is focused on the clitoris and the other on the vagina. They addressed themselves to this question in their book *Human Sexual Response:*

> Are clitoral and vaginal orgasms truly separate anatomical entities? From a biological view, the answer is an unequivocal No. The literature abounds with descriptions and discussions of vaginal as opposed to clitoral orgasms. . . . From an anatomic point of view, there is absolutely no difference in the response. . . . There may be great variation in duration and intensity of orgasmic experience, varying from individual to individual and within the same woman from time to time. However, when any woman experiences orgasmic response to effective sexual stimulation, the vagina and clitoris react in consistent psychologic patterns. Thus clitoral and vaginal orgasms are not separate biologic entities.[9]

To further bolster this discovery, Masters and Johnson also described similarities in the process of arousal and sexual gratification in women and men.

How Freud came to the conclusion that there were two distinct kinds of female orgasm makes an interesting footnote to psychosexual history that is important in disentangling the tie between vaginal orgasm and the maternal instinct. Presumably, Freud heard something from his female patients to convince him that women experienced two distinctly different kinds of orgasm. The most plausible explanation of what these women meant is suggested in a book called *Women and the Crisis in Sex Hormones,* by Barbara Seaman and Gideon Seaman. In the course of doing research on contraceptive cervical caps, they heard reports from women indicating that this method of contraception often enhanced sexual pleasure, particularly deep in the vagina. One woman was quoted in Seaman and Seaman as saying she had been very enthusiastic about a "silver pessary" that had been prescribed for her in the 1950s by a European physician. The woman remembered that the cervical cap had reduced her need for stimulation during intercourse, and she said, "I'm sure you know that in Vienna, when Freud first described the 'vaginal orgasm,' most of his women patients were using some sort of pessary or cap."[10]

Of the older, more mature—and probably, more sexually experienced—patients whom Freud saw, one assumes that if they found their way to the analytic couch, they were also likely to have found their way to a doctor who would prescribe the most sophisticated contraceptive devices available at that time. Among these was the cervical cap. Of the younger, less mature analysands, one may, in part, assume that, given the strictures on sexual behavior at that time, they were less likely to be sexually active at all and thus unlikely to have any need of contraception. But even if we operate on the theory that some people in all societies have always responded to their own desires and needs, even in the face of cultural taboos, a young, unmarried woman who was sexually active would probably still be less likely than an older, more realistic, and more sophisticated woman to obtain a cervical cap. For one thing, cervical caps had to be fitted by a physician, and young women of Freud's day, as is true of young women today, did not readily present themselves to the family doctor for contraceptive advice. Many teenagers today who have sexual relations do not ask for contraceptive advice partly because of a deep-seated reluctance to acknowledge what they are doing; they prefer to think of their lovemaking as unplanned and spontaneous activity. This must have been even more true in post-Victorian Vienna. If these suppositions are correct, and there is no reason to think they are not, it is easy to see how a metal pessary may have been responsible for Freud's misperceptions about the nature of female orgasm.

The Issue of Complementarity

Part of Freud's insistence that psychologically normal women would embrace motherhood was undoubtedly based on a belief that his theory of psychosexual development exhibited the same kind of complementarity that was so often found in nature. In many (though by no means in *all*) animal species, one sex often displays a behavior that completes or supports a related behavior in the opposite sex.

The complementarity that most concerns us was Freud's description of both sexes as parents. According to the Freudian scheme of things, a woman's primary responsibility as a parent was to nurture her young physically and emotionally, whereas a man's primary responsibility to his young was to provide for them economically. The act of providing for them economically called into play his capacity to act aggressively. Thus, as was noted earlier, men's capacity to be aggressive came to be equated with women's capacity to nurture. It was this "division of labor" in parenting that lent credence to the belief that men were, in fact, incapable of nurturing their young.

People not only accepted Freud's descriptions of femininity and masculinity, but they increasingly treated them as if they had been cast in stone. What Freud had described as complementary behavior also became mutually exclusive behavior. Each sex had its own domain, which was not to be trespassed upon by the other. Nor did the sexes permit themselves to trade off role behaviors or even to share them. To do this would have risked despoiling the by now carefully delineated cultural images of masculinity and femininity.

Ironically, as the twentieth century progressed, sex-role stereotyping regressed—to about the age of Queen Victoria, in fact. By the 1950s, the gap between masculinity and femininity was about as wide as it had ever been, and the sexes had almost become caricatures of themselves. Women did not return to the concealing dress of the Victorian era, but they did confine themselves alternately in huge, petticoated skirts or absurdly tight-fitted garments, neither of which, as was true of Victorian women, gave them any freedom of movement. As was also the case with the Victorians, domestic life in the 1950s became highly idealized. The "ideal" woman, like her Victorian counterpart, strove to be the perfect wife and mother. Men, by comparison and perhaps because of a new work ethic associated with the Industrial Revolution, emerged as even more "masculine" than their Victorian counterparts had been. The "ideal" father and husband was above all else a good provider. Men often drove themselves to heart attacks (a metaphor perhaps for what they were not otherwise permitted to do with their hearts) by focusing all their attention on their work. The head of a family was rarely to be found at his domicile, since, by definition, his masculine role required that he figuratively (and for many men, literally) work himself to death in behalf of his family.

A harmful kind of rigidity settled over the masculine and feminine roles that men and women played, almost as if each sex had put on a mask that was initially flexible but which with wearing had become hardened into one shape. It was a rigidity that denied women any opportunity for serious work apart from motherhood and housewifery, and it eliminated any possibility that men would share in any genuine caretaking of their children. This meant, in a very real sense, that a man could not acceptably display his love toward his children by nurturing them in the way that was demanded of a woman.

In the 1960s, however, when women for a variety of reasons began to broaden their sphere of activity into the traditionally masculine domain of work outside the home, an inevitable reevaluation of the established sex roles began. Women had a few problems in dealing with their newly founded careers, but basically they handled not only their careers but their expanded lives fairly well, all things considered. So people began to reason, if women could cross so easily into the traditional masculine domain, then was there any reason that men could not do the same thing and cross over into the feminine domain? Was it not, in fact, possible that men and women had been capable of both nurturing *and* careers all along but had been unable to pull off the now hardened sexual masks each was required to wear to fulfill society's expectations of them?

In mid-twentieth-century America—admittedly a far cry from Freud's world—it became almost painfully obvious that his definitions no longer worked so well, that aggression and nurturing could no longer be viewed as complementary traits. In fact, some would argue that they never had been complementary at all. The ability to act aggressively never has been the complement of nurturing behavior because it does not enable women to nurture, nor does it support them in their nurturing endeavor.

There were always other possible ways to arrange the division of labor—and love—between men and women, as a survey of many cultures would immediately have made evident, and as additional knowledge about the animal species would have proven. Instead, it took what has come to be called the sexual revolution to stir up many unanswered questions about the roles the sexes are supposed to play.

Questions that had been raised on and off since the 1890s and then quickly buried were raised again in the light of radically changing views of men's and women's psychosexual natures. For example, once again people wondered why there was no talk of womb envy as a complement to penis envy—why there were no descriptions of a paternal instinct that was truly parallel to a maternal instinct.

Karen Horney, a follower of Freud who attempted to create a separate model of feminine psychosexual development but failed to take it far enough, did write about the womb envy she observed in men she psychoanalyzed:

> When one begins, as I did, to analyze men after a fairly long experience of analyzing women, one receives a most surprising impression of the intensity of this envy of pregnancy, childbirth, and motherhood, as well as of the breasts and the act of suckling. . . . When Helene Deutsch writes that the masculinity complex in women plays a much greater part than the femininity complex in men, she would seem to overlook the fact the masculine envy is clearly capable of more successful sublimation than the penis envy of the girl, and that it certainly serves as one, if not as the essential, driving force in setting up cultural values.[11]

After years of experience observing people in many different cultures, Margaret Mead thought a paternal instinct of some sort existed, for she wrote: "No developing society that needs men to leave home and do their thing ever allows young men to handle or touch their newborns. There's always a taboo against it. For they know somewhere that, if they did, the new fathers would become so 'hooked' that they would never get out and do their 'thing' properly."[12]

There is considerable evidence to suggest that men can be nurturers. Recent studies indicate that men are just as capable of nurturing as women are and even suggest that men's failure to fulfill a parental role has deleterious effects on their children. The absence of paternal love has been linked to juvenile delinquency, excessive dependency, and homosexuality.

Less studied but more relevant to any discussion of maternal ambivalence and maternal instinct is whether men have suffered any ill effects from having been denied what might be called their paternal instinct for so many years. This may turn out to be the case, but it seems unlikely. One cannot have failed to notice that men, in fact, have carried on with their careers and that they have not appeared to suffer any serious conflict or ill effects as a result of not having been real parents to their children. Certainly, they have not suffered from the degree and variety of neuroses that have plagued women as a result of having been expected to limit themselves exclusively to motherhood. This is not to say that men are not capable or that they will not be willing participants in a more active parenting role, now that this possibility has been presented to them. Rather, it appears to be further—and perhaps final—proof that whatever the parental instinct is, it cannot be considered completely biological in origin. To the extent that it has a psychological component, the parenting instinct appears to be, at most, a reflection of a culture's current values with regard to men's and women's roles.

The really important discovery, then, especially for childless and ambivalent women, is that, however a culture may choose to define "maternal instinct" and "paternal instinct," these terms are still and always will be reflections of the current cultural value system—the cultural mandate, as it were. Any culture fluctuates in the way it defines sex roles—more or less flexibly or rigidly—depending upon the goals or needs of the culture at the moment. When sex roles are defined fairly rigidly, women who choose not to mother or to delay motherhood are frequently ostracized or made to feel uncomfortable, and in times such as the present, when sex roles are rather loosely defined, such women feel more at ease. The fact that women feel freer to remain childless is not a fantasy or distortion of reality—women *are* freer, and much of the prejudice against them has, at least for the time being, vanished, largely because fewer births are needed or even desired to maintain the population, and society is thus willing to give women freer rein with regard to reproduction. The cultural definitions of sex roles are like a pendulum, swinging first in one direction and then in another.

What remains unclear is whether the prejudice against childless women has vanished forever in Western culture. Perhaps for the first time in history, the juxtaposition of several elements and ideas makes this a real possibility. Certainly, biological knowledge has advanced to the point where no one can use science to argue that all women must mother or suffer biological consequences. A long overdue reevaluation of psychoanalytic theory is moving it in a new, enlightened direction. Women no longer need fear that they will suffer psychological damage as a result of not experiencing motherhood. Today women are encouraged to expand in whatever directions interest them, and if motherhood gets lost in their search for the right direction, well, so be it, according to many people's value systems.

Despite these changes, however, one other as yet unanalyzed force—the cultural mandate—may still remain as a barrier to genuine reproduction freedom. Just as the psychological mandate to mother shaped individual women's psyches and led to internal pressure on women to conform to society's definition of their sex role, the cultural mandate exerts a kind of collective and external pressure that is equally effective in persuading women to mother regardless of whether they have any personal inclination to do so.

10.
THE CULTURAL MANDATE: MAKING CHILDLESSNESS POSSIBLE

"Even though I know intellectually that nothing horrible will happen to me if I am never a mother, I still feel the cultural pressure to have children. There is some sense that I'm not a good citizen because I have chosen not to have children." Unlike many women who are only subliminally aware of the cultural pressure on them to become mothers, this woman seems to sense the burden placed on her by her culture. She is responding, in fact, to the cultural mandate to mother, which is the attitude that is collectively held within a culture about the role that motherhood should play in women's lives. Most of the time in most cultures, the cultural mandate is a message to women that childbearing should be their primary responsibility.

The cultural mandate plays an important role in determining how comfortable or uncomfortable a culture is with the idea that a woman has a right to choose whether or not she wants to be a mother. In cultures where few children are needed to replenish the population, women will feel more freedom to have fewer or no children, just as in cultures where population growth is a goal, women will feel more pressure to have children. Unlike biological or psychological pressures on a woman to mother, the cultural mandate has social and political overtones, and because of this, it is also the pressure that is most removed from any individual woman's control. While the biological and psychological mandates to a large extent involve internal issues that a woman can often resolve by herself, the cultural mandate consists of an external pres-

sure that does not let up, at least as long as a woman is of childbearing age.

Today most women feel that most of the pressure to have children is cultural rather than biological or psychological. When
asked if they thought there was a "maternal instinct," and, if so,
how they defined it in terms of their lives, most women interviewed
for this book described the maternal instinct as resulting almost entirely from cultural pressures on women to mother.

One young woman, who at age twenty-seven was deliberately
childless, said, "I think the maternal instinct is probably a cultural
force. I don't think it's biological. Of course, I've read things where
people say they suddenly have this biological need to have a child,
but I can't understand what that would feel like—what a biological
need to have a child would do to me. I can't relate to it. I think
what happens is, you see everyone else having babies, and you
want to do it, too. Our society seems to be set up to make women
want children. I'm sure that is why people want them."

Another woman, who, for the moment, had chosen childlessness,
commented, "I think it's cultural. If a man were put into that same
situation, he would develop the same instincts as a woman. For instance, if a woman were to die or walk out and leave her children
with their father, he would develop the same instinct to care for
them that a woman has. I do think that if a woman carries a child
in her body, something special develops, but I also think it is something that can be learned. Parenting is something that is learned
and can be developed in either sex."

Still another woman, who thought the pressure to mother was
"entirely artificial," went on to say, "I think there is perhaps a maternal instinct, but I think it is a product of our cultural learning.
Everywhere you look, women are encouraged to have babies. A lot
of the pressure is too romantic, a bit of overkill, I think. There are
so many television and magazine ads with glamorous mothers in
them. Even the diaper ads show beautiful, unharried mothers. I
remember one television show where a woman who was in her forties got pregnant. Some 'drive' just pushed her toward having that
baby, even though her husband and teenaged children thought she
shouldn't. What kind of message is that? I think that is a message
that says women should want to have every single baby they conceive. That they cannot help themselves. But then, I start to won-

der, if the maternal instinct is so strong, why do women need to be pushed to have babies anyway?"

No matter how the mandate is articulated or how a woman interprets it, few women manage to escape its message unscathed, and few women seem able to resist it entirely. The woman, then, who felt she was perhaps not being a good citizen by remaining childless was not far off the mark in her perceptions of how forceful the cultural mandate is. Not to comply with the cultural mandate to mother does indeed leave many women with an uncomfortable feeling that they are cultural outcasts or rebels.

The Cultural Mandate: Official Government Policy

In the United States, as in most cultures, the cultural mandate is shaped in large part by official policy makers rather than by women, even though they are the ones whose lives are most drastically altered by children. This means that the cultural message is delivered to all women, that is, to all the women in any one generation, since the prescribed number of children varies from generation to generation, depending upon a society's needs.

So strong is the pressure of the cultural mandate that it cannot help but influence any woman who is trying to decide whether or not she wants to have children. A woman's decision to remain childless necessarily takes on different overtones when she has to ignore a cultural expectation that she become a mother than it does when she merely has to override some part of her social learning. To do the latter is a more personal matter, which, however important to the woman, does not risk putting her at odds with her entire culture. (Individual women, of course, react in different ways to all the kinds of pressures on them to reproduce. One woman, for example, may be utterly unfazed by the notion that women are biologically programmed to have children, but may feel that she will suffer emotional harm if she does not have a child. The reverse is often true, too. A woman may not feel any psychological pressure to have a child but she may feel she is biologically pressured to do so. Only a rare woman feels no pressure of any kind to have children.)

A major problem with a cultural mandate that emanates from

official policy makers is that it often results in overwhelming pressure on women to mother. In the view of some sociologists who have observed that rigidly defined sex roles tend to occur more often when the cultural mandate is in the hands of officials rather than individuals, the cultural mandate actually amounts to a kind of cultural coercing of women into motherhood. Sociologist Judith Blake, in an article entitled "Coercive Pronatalism and American Population Policy," describes the effects of this coercion:

> In effect, regardless of whether a typical birth cohort of individuals contains a large proportion of individuals who might be unsuited to family life, human societies are organized as to attempt to make individuals as suitable as possible, to motivate them to want to be suited, and to provide them with little or no alternative to being suited as they mature. By fiction and by fiat, parenthood is the "natural" human condition, and to live one's life as a family member is the desideratum. In this context, individuals make their reproductive "choices."[1]

Although many social scientists and even women themselves have argued that an individual should be permitted to make her reproductive "choices" in an atmosphere of complete freedom, such arguments have not carried much, if any, weight with government policy makers, who often respond that permitting women this kind of freedom would cause too many women to reject motherhood entirely and that this would ultimately pose a threat to the survival of a culture.

The Politics of Childlessness

The fear that women, if left to their own devices, might not have children is the primary reason, in fact, that governments have considered the regulation of population policy to be their special province. The policy makers' fear is not totally unfounded, for as Margaret Mead wrote: "Every human society is faced with not one population problem but with two: how to beget and rear enough children and how not to beget and rear too many."[2]

Some human societies have indeed died out because they have not been able to regulate their populations, but this has not been a problem in the past few decades or even in the past century.

Today, the threat that any culture will die off because women are not having enough babies is virtually nonexistent, and indeed, most cultures suffer from the opposite problem, which is how to stabilize the population so there is no growth. Many indeed need to create a population decline in order to raise or maintain a desirable standard of living.

Despite this, governments have, for the most part, kept their strong-arm grip on birth control policy, even when their actions were not necessarily in the best interests of those whom they regulated and even when their objectives had more to do with politics than with survival. Policy makers have typically manipulated birth control policy to achieve certain sociopolitical goals, such as bolstering a declining work force, reducing unemployment, colonizing other lands, or replenishing a population after a war. At such times, the pressure on women to bear a certain number of children can be overwhelming.

To cite specific examples of government policy toward reproduction, the Soviet Union, which had been the first modern nation in 1920 to make abortion legal, made it illegal again when war with Nazi Germany was imminent, and then made it legal again after the war when extra wage earners were needed to boost the war-torn economy.[3] In the 1960s, the Japanese Government, after making abortion and the Pill accessible to women, reversed its stand and made both illegal when a declining population threatened the supply of cheap labor that was necessary to ensure Japan's growing technological dominance throughout the world.[4] In 1975 the Argentine Government prohibited the dissemination of information about birth control and restricted the sale of contraceptives in order to meet its goal of doubling its population by the end of the twentieth century.[5]

In the United States, a desire to build up the nation's industrial strength played a role in the family-oriented nature of benefits offered to World War II veterans. Low-interest loans on houses, for example, were almost entirely responsible for turning a nation of renters with the relatively low birth rates that accompany the need to rear a family in small quarters into a nation of homeowners who were willing, with government encouragement, to fill those new homes with lots of children.

Since the 1970s, the federal government has gotten even more directly involved in population policy, specifically in the area of birth control. In 1970, what had previously been unofficial government policy was signed into law with the passage of the Family Planning Services and Population Research Act. One of the stated goals of this act was to coordinate domestic population and family planning research with present and future needs of planning programs. A Special Office of Population Affairs was established within the Department of Health, Education, and Welfare. One of its mandates was to provide grants for contraceptive research—except that no grants were to be given to projects where abortion was a method of family planning.

Even the power of the Federal Drug Administration, seemingly apolitical, can be a tool for regulation of women's reproduction. For example, when the FDA recently removed cervical caps from the market for further study, despite the fact that women had been using them successfully for over 150 years, many women questioned their motivation.

At present, the government appears to be hedging its bets against the unlikely possibility that it may need population growth again, although demographers state that no population growth is desirable for the United States until well into the twenty-first century. It is more likely that official population policy planners are not entirely comfortable with the ease with which so many women are passing up motherhood. Policy makers, being only human, seem to feel the need at various periods in our history to control even women's potential for motherhood. At any rate, the current reluctance on the part of the government to support working mothers with day care and other benefits indicates a strain of pronatalism in an otherwise relatively antinatalist era. It preserves an attitude that could be used at any time to generate a social atmosphere in which all women are once again subjected to strong pressure to become mothers—and, not so coincidentally, to get out of the workplace. Unfortunately, the fact that American women have, in recent years, been given official sanction to have fewer or no children and to combine motherhood and careers but have been given so little actual social support to do so is probably no accident. Rather, it is a way for policy makers to leave the door open for the time when women will be needed to bear more children. Only when the society is reorganized to accommodate working mothers will women be guaranteed their reproductive freedom.

How effective, you may wonder, are those who manipulate so personal a matter as reproduction? The answer is very. Women appear to be far more susceptible to cultural pressure than might be supposed, particularly given the subtlety with which it is applied most of the time. In Romania, where the one-child family is the official government goal, 28 percent of all women are childless.[6] In the post-World War II United States, the birth rate quickly climbed to between three and four children per family when women were encouraged to have babies, and it dropped just as quickly to a record-setting peacetime low of fewer than 1.5 children per family during the 1960s when concerns about overpopulation became an important public issue.[7]

Even more important than how effective governments are in manipulating birth control policy is the level of coercion they use, if necessary, to get women to mother. This has often been a destructive force in many women's lives. Since the 1960s, though, the United States and the rest of the Western world has been in a relatively antinatalist mood, brought on, as just noted, by fears that the population was too large to support itself and maintain the high standard of living that Westerners had grown accustomed to. Other factors creating a mood of antinatalism were a twenty-year decline in the world economy, the demands of women for greater social and economic equality, a restructuring of family life that is currently under way (in large part because of the changes in women's status), and an unprecedented concern for the quality of life that is tied to the environmentalist movement. Women have, as a result, been freer to have smaller families than in the past and even to have no children if that is what they wanted. Certainly, to have an only child has become acceptable in a way that it never was before.

Such an atmosphere, unfortunately, may have lulled women into thinking they have in fact obtained a measure of reproductive freedom, when they have merely been the beneficiaries of a relatively antinatalist cycle in the cultural mandate. Should the cultural mandate swing into a more conservative, pronatalist cycle, once again, married women will undoubtedly find themselves coerced in many ways to have children. And as has happened in the past, cultural disapproval may be directed toward childless women. But they will also be especially vulnerable, because, for the first time ever, many women have publicly announced their intentions to remain childless. This makes them especially visible targets.

Such a swing could be brought on by many factors—continued high unemployment; a reassessment of cultural values, particularly with regard to family life and women's roles; or simply by a kind of amorphous uneasiness over the fact that women are not having many children. (The race-suicide war of the early 1900s, after all, during which much criticism was directed toward childless women, as described in Chapter 7, was not based on any real need to increase the birth rate, but rather, on backlash prompted by the observation that the birth rate among the "best women," i.e., white, upper- and middle-class women, was considerably lower than among immigrant and black women.) Enormous pressure could be brought to bear on all women, and childless women could, once again, become the special targets. They might become, in effect, what Mead has referred to as society's "witches":

> The figure of the witch who kills living things, who strokes the throat of children till they die, whose very glance causes cows to lose their calves and fresh milk to curdle as it stands, is a statement of human fear of what can be done to mankind by a woman who denies or is forced to deny child-bearing, child-cherishing.[8]

Revising the Cultural Mandate: The Case for Free Choice

What the witch symbolized historically—a cultural metaphor for the childless woman—she could come to represent once again if the cultural mandate is not revised to ensure the reproductive freedom of all women all the time, and not just in times like the present when a low population is desired. Preventing backlash against childless women may be the single most important reason to take steps to ensure that the cultural mandate is rewritten to support the new lives so many women are creating for themselves. This can only be done by instituting a new cultural mandate that guarantees each woman the freedom to choose, first, whether she will have any children, and second, how many children she will bear.

An obvious question is why women have not simply grabbed the reins and taken over control of their own reproductive lives. The major, and until recently unsurmountable, reason they have not done this is that for centuries there was little that a woman could do to prevent herself from conceiving. Only with the development of the Pill did women finally have a method for controlling the number of births, but even this relatively safe and failure-proof method is not in the hands of women. The distribution of the Pill, and certain other kinds of contraception as well, remains in the hands of official policy makers, who can deny women the use of the Pill or any other contraceptive, including abortion, simply by declaring it unsafe and removing it from the market; by making it available to some women (married women) but not to others (unmarried women); or by manipulating public opinion against it.

Then, too, women have not created their own cultural mandate in part because motherhood is not without its own rewards, something that those who attempt to turn childlessness into a social or political movement would do well to keep in mind. For many women, motherhood is still a primary source of identification and fulfillment. Over half of all mothers may now work, but that still leaves a sizable minority at home and involved in full-time motherhood. Of the mothers who do work outside the home, many hold jobs only out of economic necessity and work at jobs that can hardly be considered careers. Of those who have careers, many consciously permit their careers to take a back seat to motherhood for a number of years. After all, as chastised as women have been for not bearing children, they also have frequently been elevated to a pedestal when they did. Giving this up without something very meaningful to take its place would for many women be an intolerable exchange.

Today, however, women increasingly have other resources through which they can develop a strong identity. Some women have found in their careers a source of identification that can equal, and for some, surpass, motherhood, and more women will find this to be true in the future. Furthermore, in most families, two incomes have become necessary. Even if the policy makers were to decide that women should once again go home and make babies, few families would be able to tolerate this purely on financial grounds. These combined factors mean that the birth rate in the United States is liable to remain low throughout the rest of the twentieth century, barring war.

For all these reasons, many people have begun to suggest that the official policy makers no longer act in the best interests of those for whom they create policy, and that it is time for governments to get out of the population-control business, thereby permitting women to make their reproductive choices in an atmosphere of total freedom. Indeed, people may already be claiming the right to make their own choices. The environmental movement, which includes groups dedicated to little or no population growth, is perhaps the single most important grass-roots action to emerge in the United States in this century, and reproductive freedom is an important aspect of it.

The demand for reproductive freedom for women, however, has been growing since the first feminist movement began after the Civil War, and women's activities for equal rights have played a significant role in laying the groundwork for reproductive freedom. In 1916, Leta Hollingworth, a pioneer feminist and clinical psychologist, described the time when women would demand the right to choose how many, if any, children they would bear:

> The time is coming and is indeed almost at hand, when all the most intelligent women of the community, who are the most desirable child-bearers, will become conscious of the methods of social control. The type of normality will be questioned; the laws will be changed . . . illusions will fade away and give place to clearness of view. . . . The natural desire for children may, and probably will, always guarantee a stationary population, even if child-bearing becomes a voluntary matter.[9]

As for the objections that have been raised among women themselves, those who claim that the right to choose childlessness would diminish the role of motherhood in all women's lives actually have little to fear, for as Jessie Bernard has so astutely noted, there would be advantages for everyone:

> Nonmotherhood also promises gains for the women we have called "nestlings"; the women who want many babies. . . . By

foregoing motherhood themselves, some women would make available to the nestlings the "privilege" of having more children than the "permitted" two. Every woman who "surrendered" the privilege of bearing her "quota" of two would make it "permissible" for another woman to have four.[10]

The most important benefit of the right to choose whether or not to have children, however, would not accrue to mothers or even to those women who had already decided to remain childless, but rather, it would help the women who are currently caught in the quandary of maternal ambivalence—who find themselves hopelessly caught up in issues and unable to make a decision either way. These women would be able to make their decisions in an atmosphere that was, at least, free of external pressures. One hopes their decisions would only be healthier and more realistic for having been made in such an atmosphere.

11.
CHILDLESS
BY CHOICE

Rewriting the cultural mandate to include genuine reproductive freedom, unfortunately, is not so simple a matter as women taking control of what is rightfully theirs to control, anyway. While the cultural mandate is largely determined by official policy, the actual manipulation of that policy might best be seen as a sort of fine-tuning operation. For example, if a government needed almost every woman to have three children in order to reach a certain level of population growth, the public policy makers, mostly working through the mass media, would persuade most women to have three children. The overall picture, though, namely, that of convincing women that they have a social responsibility to reproduce in the first place, is achieved through a far more complex process known as socialization.

In our society, the task of socializing both sexes mostly falls on the mother's shoulders. It is part of the cultural teaching about sex roles that goes on in varying degrees in all cultures, and it begins, in most instances, at the moment of birth.

Even very young children are aware of the behavior that is expected of them with regard to their sexes. Although the fact that sex-role training is an important part of one's cultural indoctrination is recognized, the specifics of how little children learn to want to be mothers or fathers is still somewhat shrouded in mystery. Many people, though, have attempted to devise theories to explain the process or to provide details of how children are influenced by their cultural learning. Only when this process is uncovered will we be able to change the cultural values regarding motherhood and childlessness in any meaningful way.

One hindrance to doing research about sex roles, however, is the fact that results of the data that has been compiled are contradictory and often unclear. The subject of sex roles is still so unexplored in some respects that there may yet be some major discoveries to be made with regard to differences and similarities between the sexes. Despite this, there is nowhere else to look for possible keys to changing the cultural mandate and even for explanations of the kind of maternal ambivalence that so many women are experiencing today.

Teaching Girls to Want Motherhood: The Mother's Role

Nancy Chodorow, whose seminal book *The Reproduction of Mothering* presents a new view of how women are socialized into motherhood, observed that as boys and girls are reared, they either must receive different treatment from their mothers or they must perceive that this is what happens.[1] Some differences in how children are reared, nearly all experts agree, are needed to account for the fact that, in Western culture at least, parenting involves one set of responsibilities for men and another for women. Chodorow has stated: "Women come to mother because they have been mothered by women. By contrast, that men are mothered by women reduces their parenting capacities."[2] A now familiar corollary to this might be: to prepare women for their parenting role, they are taught to nurture babies and small children. By contrast, to prepare men for their parenting role, they are taught to want to go out in the world and earn a living so they can support their families.

When one looks for the differences in how girls and boys are reared that explain the differences in parental responsibilities between the sexes, however, there are far fewer than might be expected. In *The Psychology of Sex Differences*, a massive review of over 2,000 studies on sex differences, many of which involved very young children, Eleanor Maccoby and Carol Jacklin found that there seemed to be few actual differences in how preschool youngsters were treated by their mothers.[3] For example, when researchers anticipated that they might find that mothers tended to talk more to girls than to boys or that they maintained differing sets of expectations about educational achievement, this proved not to be the case.[4] But when researchers turned their attention to the differences that did exist, some information emerged that may be particularly relevant to maternal ambivalence.

In general, since females are taught to nurture, one would expect them to receive more physical affection than males do. A study with rhesus monkeys showed that this is indeed the case. Mothers do tend to fondle female babies more than male babies. What is even more relevant, however, is the way they tend to play more with male babies than with female babies.[5] Studies done with humans are too mixed to show definite results, but girls report perceiving that they receive more affection than boys do. On the other hand, roughhouse play with boys is also more encouraged than with girls by both parents.[6]

Another important area where differences might be expected to emerge in how boys and girls are reared is the amount of autonomy that a mother encourages. Presumably, boys would be encouraged to develop more autonomy and independence than girls would because they are viewed as being more autonomous and independent as adults. Furthermore, one of the qualifications of a mother is that she must be able to undergo periods of relatively little autonomy as she devotes most of her time and energy to caring for a totally helpless infant. Among preschool youngsters, however, there appear to be no differences in the amount of autonomy that mothers encourage. Autonomy, in fact, does not even appear to be an issue except to the degree that it suits a mother's convenience. Mothers do not differentiate between the sexes in such matters as how far or how much they permit a child to roam from home, encouraging a child to dress itself, or the setting of bedtimes. In fact, they tend to encourage autonomy in these and other matters only if it makes their lives easier; they discourage it where it does not.[7]

As children get older, though, mothers do behave differently toward boys and girls. And the behavior is especially interesting for what it says about women's lives today. Surprisingly, as children get older, mothers tend to permit girls more freedom and autonomy than they do boys.[8] Equally surprisingly, mothers tend to restrict boys physically more than girls, although one would expect the reverse to be true.[9] Finally, mothers tend to punish boys more than they do girls. One researcher found that mothers reported having more difficulty punishing their daughters than their sons.[10] In fact, this appears to be a cultural prejudice. In research done with college students, subjects showed greater reluctance to administer electric shock to girls than to boys.[11]

The last area where differences in the sexes might be expected to reflect training for parenthood is that of aggressive behavior. Although little subtle research has been done on aggressive behavior and despite the fact that parents deny that they would let a child of either sex act aggressively toward playmates, when such behavior does occur, it is tolerated more in boys than in girls.[12] An unusually aggressive little girl soon gets the message that her behavior is not considered feminine. But in the case of little boys, a double message is sent. They are first warned against aggressive behavior and then carefully watched to make sure they display an appropriate amount of it. In interviews, fathers admitted worrying more about the lack of aggressive behavior in their sons than in their daughters.[13]

The Result: Maternal Ambivalence

From all these seemingly unrelated facts, a hint of a pattern emerges. It is a pattern from which a theory of maternal ambivalence can be inferred. For a moment, even though there is great truth in it, ignore Chodorow's theory that mothers socialize their sons by reducing their capacities to parent and focus on the corollary, namely, that mothers tend to prepare their sons for the workplace as a way of socializing them for parenthood. Working to support a family, after all, is part of the cultural definition of fatherhood in most of the Western world. Furthermore, consider that most gainful work is done outside the home and under fairly restrictive circumstances—a worker, whether he be an employee or the owner of a company, cannot simply roam away from his job during the day as his whims dictate. To succeed, a man needs a great deal of self-discipline—the kind that is acquired, perhaps, through his socialization. That boys are punished more than girls and subjected to greater physical restriction may in fact be excellent training for their roles as fathers, as we shall see later. Little boys learn at an early age that certain physical restrictions on them will be necessary to achieve success and earn money. Roughhouse play, or, for that matter, any kind of play, may be a way of teaching males how to get along with others in competitive situations. A certain amount of healthy aggression also serves a person well in competitive situations. By instilling certain traits—the ability to concentrate, the ability to stay in one place for a long time, the ability to compete—in their sons, mothers prepare them to handle their responsibilities.

As we have seen, little girls are generally not subject to the same conditioning as little boys. And it is because of this that they are suited for their relatively free, unstructured—or at any rate, self-structured—lives as mothers and housewives. The fact that girls perceive that they receive more affection than boys may contribute to their ability as nurturers, but the fact that they are not played with the roughhouse way that boys are undoubtedly contributes to their inability to compete as well as men do in the workplace. That most girls are not restricted physically or even punished very often compared to boys may help to create the kind of temperament that makes them especially well suited to be mothers. Mothering involves a great deal of spontaneous physical activity, especially compared to the restrictions that are placed on almost all other workers. That women are trained to be less aggressive than men also may be a limiting factor in their ability to compete in the workplace.

Until recently, when certain elements of society began to question the division of sex roles, these differences in conditioning served everyone quite well. It is important to realize, however, that this division of sexual labor has not been with us for all time, and that, in fact, it only emerged about two hundred years ago in response to the changing pattern of family life during the Industrial Revolution.

Prior to the Industrial Revolution, both men and women were, in a very real sense, gainfully employed in their homes. A man worked as a farmer or planter, or he operated a small shop or business, which was usually attached to his dwelling. A woman was fully occupied with the arduous work that was involved in making nearly everything her family needed to subsist. We can infer from this physical setup that husband and wife probably shared in the parenting, particularly once a child was past infancy. Whether the child care was truly shared equally, or whether the larger portion of it fell to the woman, is irrelevant; what matters is that it was shared, particularly in contrast to the pattern of parenting that emerged later.

Three important changes brought about by the Industrial Revolution, however, caused a shift in this division of sexual labor. First, the Industrial Revolution took work out of the home, and men went with it. (Actually, poor women also left the home, largely to work in factories.) This left women—at least middle- and upper-class women—in the home. Second, many products that had formerly been made in the home were now made in factories and several new inventions for the home considerably lightened the work load of women. Third, and most important for purposes of this discussion, a new pattern of parenting emerged. Women, at least middle- and upper-class women, were expected to stay home. The primary focus of their lives became their children. In fact, women's real work had now become the nurturing of their children. By contrast, men were no longer available to share the parenting in the way that they had been when they, too, did their work at home. Men's work outside the home eventually left them with little time for anything but the most perfunctory of relationships with their children.

Naturally, as men's and women's sex roles were redefined, the way they were socialized changed, too. Women were no longer prepared, in a social sense, for the work of running a self-sustaining household, nor were they taught any of the social skills they might need to work outside their homes. Men no longer learned or were expected to nurture. Increasingly, the social skills they needed to acquire to assure them of success in the workplace included such things as the ability to compete, mental toughness, and ambition.

Where men and women before the Industrial Revolution had been socialized so that their skills and personal traits were overlapping to some degree, as the new sex roles took hold, the socialization of the sexes more and more involved the teaching of skills that were mutually exclusive. This was especially true with regard to parenting. As noted in the previous chapter, a woman's role as a parent was to nurture her children physically and emotionally, whereas a man's role as a parent was more or less one of providing financial support.

Today, though, as was also noted in the previous chapter, the mutual exclusivity with which both sexes are socialized has begun to create problems. The rigid lines of parental responsibility that were drawn approximately two centuries ago have begun to crumble. Fathers have started showing an interest in nurturing their children, even if they do not initially do it as well as women do. The skills that were ingrained in women from an early age must be acquired at a later stage by fathers, but this men are managing to do quite well.

Similarly, women today expect to lead lives that include work outside the home and even to relinquish some of the nurturing. This is a relatively new role for women, however, and the majority of women have not been socialized for it. It comes as no surprise, then, that women, like men trying out nurturing, have encountered some special problems in handling their new, expanded roles. The Superwoman syndrome is one of the more obvious attempts to cope, but the fact that women do not achieve as much success in the workplace as men do is perhaps the biggest price they pay for their present social conditioning.

Hardly anyone can have failed to notice that however many rights women have obtained and however many doors have been opened to them, they still lag behind their male counterparts, not only because real prejudice continues to hinder their progress, but also in ways that can only be accounted for by the way they have been socialized—or, as appears to be the case, by the way they have not been socialized. Women's conflicts over work and motherhood seem to be as much related to what they have not learned as to what they have. Most important, a woman's inability to achieve the traditional male-oriented success in her career is tied to her feelings of maternal ambivalence.

Malkah Notman, among others, has noted that women—even highly ambivalent women—have a tendency to opt for motherhood when they are faced with a crucial turning point in their careers:

> Becoming pregnant, deliberately or inadvertently, may be a way of avoiding difficulties within a career, or an expression of anxiety a woman faces at the point where she is about to make an important move. It is not uncommon to encounter women who were about to return to graduate school or start work on

a long-delayed book or other project, who then become pregnant.[14]

But this should not be seen as too surprising a development if a woman's life has been shaped as much by what she has not been taught as by what she has. What may look like a cop-out on the part of a well-educated, well-trained professional woman may actually be a rather confusing inability to come to terms with, or recognize, that her work problems—and the maternal ambivalence that nearly always surfaces at this time—may be related to the fact that she has not been socialized to succeed in her professional endeavors. If the climb to the top seems harder for her, despite seemingly equal opportunities, it is, for reasons that have little to do with her training, education, or experience and everything to do with her sex-role socialization. Confusion often results when a woman fails to recognize that she is caught in a cultural trap—and that out of that confusion comes the maternal ambivalence so many women are experiencing today.

The Solutions: Motherhood, Careers, and More Ambivalence

In a sense, it would be abnormal for young women today not to experience some maternal ambivalence given their cultural training. It is hardly surprising that a generation of women caught in a tumultuous era of changing sex roles would experience ambivalence over both their work and motherhood. When the ambivalence does strike, a woman with the same—or more—education and experience as a male peer often cannot manage to sort out why he is about to be made vice president or senior partner and she is not, and she may consciously or unconsciously turn to something she is quite prepared to do: motherhood.

But this is a rather convoluted path to motherhood, one that really solves nothing and often only adds to a woman's frustration later on. Having gotten a taste of one world but having been socialized into another, most women today find themselves wanting both worlds. And in wanting both worlds, women also are finding themselves repulsed by both. A woman fears that if she commits to one choice, the other may then be closed off or much harder to obtain. For many women, this results in a kind of paralysis, a period of being endlessly obsessed about whether a career or motherhood is the right choice, whether both are possible, and which is to be given up if both are not. This is the heart of the kind of maternal ambivalence women are experiencing today.

One woman, age twenty-four, in describing the pain of her ambivalence, commented, "I wish I could decide once and for all to have a baby, or even figure out whether I want one. Then I could plan the rest of my life. Even making the wrong mistake might be better than this state of indecisiveness I'm in. One day I'm so absorbed by my career that I think I can't possibly have a child. Then the next day, I'm staring somewhat jealously at pregnant women. I see mothers and babies everywhere. It looks good to me. But I always scare myself away before I actually do anything about it."

Another woman, age thirty and a painter, described her struggle with ambivalence: "I feel that I will have to give up my work if I have a baby. And it's too important to me for that to happen. Recently, though, I talked with a friend who had a child about two years ago after working for about ten years on her career. I brought up my fears, and asked if she had ever had them. She said, 'If you have a baby, you'll give up some of your paintings, but you won't give all of them up.' That made me feel better for a while, but then, my old fears returned. They always do. I don't think my friend ever felt as much ambivalence as I do. Perhaps she was always more willing to give up whatever she had to in order to have a baby. She always had more faith that she could work and be a mother."

Many women live for several years or more in the kind of limbo this ambivalence provokes. Some women continue until the decision is taken out of their hands, and they can no longer have children anyway. For other women, however, the situation becomes intolerable. The pressures mount—from their spouses, their bosses, their families, their cultures, or within themselves—to the point where a woman feels she must take some action, any action, that will relieve her of her maternal ambivalence. One way or another, the woman takes a plunge.

Women who feel more ambivalent about their careers than about motherhood will find motherhood an easier solution to maternal ambivalence. They more or less retreat into motherhood. Unfortunately, for everyone involved, though, this too often results in a kind of ambivalent motherhood, a motherhood by default that bodes ill for the mother or the child, and often for both.

An increasingly popular solution today, however, given the pressure on women to combine motherhood and work, is to decide on childlessness, even if temporarily, but often permanently. This way, all a woman's energies can be directed toward her career, and her chances for achieving professional success are, in fact, increased.

How a woman does in either situation depends on her personal makeup and her sense of self-awareness, but the woman who opts for motherhood may not really have resolved her problem with maternal ambivalence. Nor necessarily has the woman who decides to pour her energies into her career—like the woman who becomes an ambivalent mother, she will also continue to struggle with her ambivalence. It can be put on a back burner for a few months or even for a few years, but eventually, it will return to haunt her, often at the very time when she is most vulnerable—just as her childbearing years are running out.

A last-minute resolution of maternal ambivalence by deciding to have a child may look like a good and even natural solution, especially when time is running out, but too often it is not any better a solution than choosing childlessness. Too many women believe they are choosing motherhood because it is truly what they want to do, when, in fact, they are really using motherhood to avoid career problems. The very fact that a woman has been postponing motherhood for ten or fifteen years is often testimony to how deep-seated her maternal ambivalence is—and how unlikely it is to be erased by a last-minute leap into motherhood. Sometimes, however, it does work; there are many women for whom the last-minute decision to mother is right. But there are also many women for whom it is not.

For example, one woman, who had her first and only child at age thirty-eight, after finding out that she was not going to be made a senior partner in her law firm, described her difficulties in coping with her decision: "I thought I had my baby because I was swept away with maternal feeling, and I was, in fact, consumed with the idea that it was now or never because of my age. I would not for a minute say that motherhood does not have its rewards or that I don't love my child and consider her one of the great blessings of my life, but it hasn't been easy. I do miss my job, and I feel I ran out on problems I could have solved. I often resent the fact that I'm not going to the office with everyone else in the morning. I feel like everyone in the world but me goes off to work. And I'm frustrated that I cannot make everything at home run as efficiently as my office. I'm a problem solver, but my baby doesn't seem to know that. Or maybe she does, and takes great delight in imposing her schedule on mine. At any rate, it's been difficult."

Another woman, who became a first-time mother at forty-one, remarked, "I got pregnant accidentally, believe it or not. I had stopped being so careful with birth control because I thought I wasn't very likely to conceive at my age. That alone is a solution to ambivalence that I could discuss for hours, but I won't. I thought it was a message from heaven or a reprieve or something along those lines. I mean, our whole society is so mystical about motherhood, and I was willing to buy into it.

"Well, even though I love my son, and he has added to my life in ways I never would have guessed, I have to admit I'm an ambivalent mother. I decided to stay home for a year, but after three months I was eager to go back to work. Now there are days when I can't wait for five o'clock to roll around so I get home to him. But there are also other days when that hour rolls around and I'm not done at work and I just don't want to leave, even though I have to, and do. I know what this is all about. I have become just as ambivalent a mother as I was a childless woman. Only frankly, I worry more about it now since it can possibly affect my child. I also sometimes think there's nothing I can do about it except live with it."

If burying the ambivalent feelings in either motherhood or a career does not work, facing up to them is a solution that often does. For one thing, it can open many avenues of emotional support to a woman. As women have learned in so many other areas of their lives, there is comfort in sharing problems, and the problem of maternal ambivalence is one that almost every young woman experiences to one degree or another today.

Facing up to the ambivalence also helps a woman avoid the trap of indefinitely postponing motherhood. The idea that a woman can safely postpone childbearing, which, thanks to advances in medical science, she can do for a longer period today than even ten years ago, is one that has taken hold of women today perhaps to a detrimental extent. It has falsely provided many women with the notion that they need not even attempt to resolve their ambivalence, but rather, that they can let it resolve itself over time.

Unfortunately, something else also resolves itself with the passage of time and that is the ability to conceive. Conception becomes much more difficult. On the average, a woman who easily may conceive within about six months when she is twenty-five may find that as many as one to two years are required for conception at age forty. Although some controversy exists over this, a great deal of evidence points to the fact that a woman's fertility begins to decline, although only slightly according to some reports, after about age thirty or even as early as twenty-seven, depending upon which expert you want to believe.

What are the implications for an ambivalent woman? For one, a woman who has postponed having children into her late thirties probably may not have left enough time for her physician to identify and correct any fertility problem she may have if she decides to have a child, after all. Similarly, a woman with a deep-seated emotional problem over motherhood or childlessness will find that time is running out on her, too. While the potential for changing one's behavior always exists, the years of therapy that may be required to do so also erode the childbearing years. Postponing children, even temporarily, is an expression of maternal ambivalence that may not be easily resolved, and that certainly may not be resolved in a short time. This is something no woman who may want to have children can afford to ignore.

For all these reasons, a woman experiencing maternal ambivalence, regardless of her age, should not treat it as a casual problem or an open-ended decision that will resolve itself. A woman who finds herself unable—or psychologically unwilling—to deal with her maternal ambivalence after several months, a year, or at most two years of thinking about it may want to get outside help in confronting her feelings and sorting out what they mean.

Increasingly, for many women, the resolution to maternal ambivalence will be childlessness. Quite simply, it makes sense for many women today. If a woman can resolve the personal and interpersonal issues that are tied to her ambivalence, she may find that she is comfortable having no children. For a large number of women—25 percent of all women in their twenties, as one expert has predicted—to be comfortable with childlessness, however, one more thing must be resolved. The current cultural message that all women must be on call for, if not actually engaged in, motherhood must change, because no matter how much any individual woman does to resolve her personal ambivalence, women still will not be free to choose childlessness unless they are also free of the cultural pressure.

And for the cultural pressure to be eradicated, something else must happen, and it must begin, in part, with the way that women are socialized to want to mother, as well as with the way they are socialized against traditional career success. Only when the socialization process itself is changed will the cultural mandate be one that truly guarantees genuine reproductive choice to women.

Fortunately, socialization into a sex role is not a fixed process; it varies with the times and even from culture to culture. As the way that women are indoctrinated into their sex roles is expanded to provide a wider range of options, so, too, will the possibilities of women's lives be expanded. The cultural mandate will inevitably change at the same time. Only then will women learn that they truly do have choices about how to live their lives—that they can combine motherhood and careers, that they can have many children if that is what they want, and that they can freely choose childlessness, too.

CONCLUSION:
A PERSONAL VIEW

A friend who had her first child at age thirty-six and who at age thirty-nine was weighing whether or not to have another child told me of the pressure she received from her gynecologist not to have a second child. His argument consisted solely of the following statement: "Think how old you will be when the child is in high school." Had he been her physician when she was considering whether to have her first child, he undoubtedly would have dissuaded her from that, too, presumably to save yet another child from the social embarrassment of "older" parents.

As she told me this story, I recalled myself ten years earlier, sitting in my gynecologist's office right after my annual examination. I was twenty-seven. My mother was twenty-seven when she had me, her first child, but I had not yet connected my rather sudden and certainly alarming attack of discontent with this fact. All I knew was that I was enjoying a wonderful career and dating exciting if somewhat erratic and undependable men. All our energies went into our careers, and they were no more inclined to marry me than I was to marry them. I was even less inclined to have children. Despite this, I had somehow absorbed enough of the cultural teachings of the time to sense that time was fleeting, that perhaps I *should want* to settle down, get married, and have children. "Why," I half-wailed to my doctor, "don't I want to settle down? Why don't I want to be a mother? Is it getting to be too late? When will I be too old?"

Unlike my friend's physician, mine was a true healer of the mind as well as the body. He was also a man ahead of his time. He reassured me by telling me that lots of women felt as I did, that there was no "right time" to have children, that for some women there was never any time to have them. He further consoled me by pointing out that my grandmothers had probably borne children well into their forties, that women did not need to have children as early as they had been encouraged to do in recent years. This wise man shared all this with me even before there was widespread acceptance of late motherhood and childlessness, even before the medical establishment had discovered techniques and tests that made motherhood into a woman's forties safer than it had been for any previous generation.

Having read this far, you undoubtedly think that I am going to make one last point in favor of childlessness. That I am going to reassure you that ambivalence is just something to be lived with for however long it takes you to decide what it is you truly want out of life. I think that I need not make any other points in favor of childlessness, having, I hope, done that in the preceding pages. I fully and firmly believe that some women have little inclination to mother small children and that they should not feel pressure of any kind to do so. Alternately, I support late motherhood. I think there are great joys in motherhood at any age, and even special ones that accrue to women who have their children later than the norm. I have watched my friends and acquaintances take on motherhood in their late thirties and early forties with as much grace and vigor as any younger women have, and with, I might add, a measure of sympathy and maturity that is often lacking in younger women. These are not—or at least should not be—matters of cultural taste. I believe in reproductive freedom for women and feel that it can only be achieved by accepting that there are many possible ways for people to lead their lives.

On the subject of maternal ambivalence, I am, however, concerned that I will be viewed as condoning maternal ambivalence rather than a woman's right to choose whether or not to reproduce. After having learned so much about pregnancy and childbirth while doing the research for this book, I cannot in good faith advise any women to ignore the ambivalence or to drift with it for a few years to see if it does not resolve itself.

An ambivalent woman, after all, is a woman who still might decide to have a child. And that is something, unfortunately, that women can do only until a certain age. It is something that a woman does at increasing risk to herself and her child as she gets older. I even believe—and there is some scientific evidence to support my belief—that the father's age is a major risk factor in reproduction at a later age. There is ample evidence to support the belief that people were meant to have babies at a young age— for biological reasons, if for no other. Medical science has pushed the age for safe childbearing forward in recent years, and it is my fervent, and I believe, not unrealistic hope that modern medical science will find a way to prolong the childbearing years still more.

I think there is absolutely nothing emotionally or psychologically to prevent a woman from becoming a mother at any age, just as I believe that no harm will befall a woman who decides she does not want any children. But there is a biological time clock that none of us can escape, and it is because of this that I cannot in good conscience encourage women to live with their ambivalence until a solution presents itself, which is exactly what many women are doing today. Rather, I think that women who find themselves unable to decide whether or not they want a child should examine the issues as well as their own lives—in short, they should do everything possible to resolve their ambivalence.

Unfortunately, ambivalence over whether or not to have a child has become something of a fashionable subject, good fodder for intimate talks among female friends and Sunday afternoon rap sessions with one's mate, a chic topic of conversation at dinner parties in some circles. Women receive lots of encouragement today not to have children until they have done the other things they want to do with their lives—until they are absolutely ready to become mothers. And this is as it should be. For the sake of mother and child, ambivalence is best resolved before you become a mother, since it does not necessarily go away afterward.

Apart from the fact that time runs out for a woman biologically, there are other reasons not to treat the ambivalence as an open-ended decision. From my conversations with women who have decided on childlessness and women who were in varying stages of dealing with their ambivalence, from my research, and from my personal experience, I have come to the conclusion that it is impossible to be fully engaged in a career, in other interests, perhaps in

deep relationships, and even in life itself without first having resolved this important question as much as possible.

Recently I asked another friend whether she wanted any children. Despite our closeness during the time I was writing this
book, she had never confided her views about childlessness to me.
My curiosity had grown, and from interviewing so many women, I
had learned that the best way to elicit personal information is to
ask a direct question, so I did. My friend responded with something that I had heard possibly hundreds of times over the three
years it took me to write this book. She said she could not decide
whether or not she wanted a child since she was not involved with
a man. It was a decision she had decided to put off until she got
involved with someone whom she might marry.

That would have been my answer until I became involved in the
research and writing of this book. It is a very self-justifying response: you have this problem, but you cannot solve it until you do
something else, so you have given yourself permission to do nothing. Yet, in the course of my writing, I had no choice but to consider whether I wanted a child. I had to face the issues, compare
myself with other women in various stages of ambivalence. Man or
no man in my life, I had to deal with this issue. I even came to realize that knowing whether or not I wanted a child would have an
effect on the kind of men I would become involved with.

What I decided is irrelevant; *that* I decided is what really matters. That all women of childbearing age should take at least the
initial steps toward resolving their feelings of maternal ambivalence is something I have become convinced of during the writing
of this book.

I do not think that, deep inside, women are comfortable with the
ambivalence they are feeling these days toward motherhood. I do
not think avoiding the issues is healthy. Furthermore, there are a
great many things to be considered, and this itself will take time. A
woman in any kind of holding pattern with regard to whether or
not she wants to be a mother is only wasting what I have come to
regard as highly valuable time. She needs to think about the role
her career will play, as well as the role motherhood will play, in
her life; the kind of partner, if any, she is seeking; how she relates
to her own mother (a matter of no small concern in how a woman
mothers); how she views herself as a woman. Almost never is the

question of whether or not one wants to be a mother easily resolved. Months, and often years, may be required to work out the ambivalent feelings toward motherhood or to come to terms with the fact that they cannot be resolved and that childlessness is the solution. The sooner a woman starts to sort out this issue, the sooner she can get on with her life.

Notes

CHAPTER 1

1. Stephanie Mills, "The Future Is a Cruel Hoax," in Ellen Peck and Judith Senderowitz, eds., *Pronatalism* (New York: Crowell, 1974), pp. 270–71.
2. Ellen Peck, *The Baby Trap* (New York: Pinnacle, 1972).
3. Ann Landers, column, Chicago *Sun-Times*, March 29, 1976.
4. Maria W. Piers, *Infanticide: Past and Present* (New York: Norton, 1978), p. 37.

CHAPTER 2

1. Edward Pohlman, "Childlessness, Intentional and Unintentional: Psychological and Sociological Aspects," *Journal of Nervous Disorders* 151 (1970): 2–12.
2. Erik H. Erikson, "Inner Space and Outer Space: Reflections on Womanhood," *Daedalus* (1964): 590.
3. Erikson, quoted in the New York *Times*, August 4, 1979, Section A.
4. Carl Lichtman, "Voluntary Childlessness: A Thematic Analysis of the Person and the Process," (Ed.D. diss., Columbia University Teachers College, 1976), p. 18.
5. Ibid., pp. 23–24.
6. Ibid.
7. Lee Hersh, "Self-Actualization as It Relates to the Decision To Have Children," unpublished paper, 1974.
8. Lichtman, "Voluntary Childlessness," p. 27.
9. Ibid.

10. Jean Veevers, "Voluntarily Childless Wives: An Exploratory Study," *Sociology and Social Research* 57 (April 1973): 356–66.

11. Lois Wladis Hoffman, "The Professional Woman as Mother," in Ruth B. Kundsin, ed., *Women & Success: The Anatomy of Achievement* (New York: Morrow, 1974), p. 224.

12. Caryl Rivers, Rosalind Barnett, and Grace Baruch, *Beyond Sugar and Spice: How Women Grow, Learn, and Thrive* (New York: Putnam, 1979), p. 87.

13. Cynthia Epstein, personal interview.

14. Lichtman, "Voluntary Childlessness," pp. 68–69.

15. Jean Veevers, "The Moral Careers of Voluntarily Childless Wives: Notes on the Defense of a Variant World View," *The Family Coordinator* 24 (1975): 473–87.

16. Lichtman, "Voluntary Childlessness," p. 59.

17. Ibid., p. 48.

18. Cynthia Epstein, personal interview.

19. Epstein, personal interview.

20. Lichtman, "Voluntary Childlessness," p. 31.

21. Ibid., p. 69.

22. Veevers, "Moral Careers," pp. 473–87.

23. Veevers, "Voluntarily Childless Wives," pp. 356–66.

24. Lichtman, "Voluntary Childlessness," p. 83.

25. Ibid., p. 57.

26. Judith Bardwick, *Psychology of Women: A Study in Bio-Cultural Conflicts* (London: Harper & Row, 1971).

27. Judith Guss Teicholz, "Psychological Correlates of Voluntary Childlessness in Married Women," paper presented at the Eastern Psychological Association, March 1978.

28. Veevers, "Voluntarily Childless Wives," pp. 356–66.

CHAPTER 3

1. E. E. LeMasters, "Parenthood as a Crisis," *Marriage and Family Living* 19 (November 1957): 352–55.

2. Alice Rossi, "Transition to Parenthood," *Journal of Marriage and the Family* 30 (February 1968): 28.

3. Ibid., p. 27.

4. LeMasters, "Parenthood as a Crisis," p. 354.

5. Ibid., p. 353.
6. Ibid.
7. Rossi, "Transition," pp. 30, 35–36.
8. Angus Campbell et al., *The Quality of American Life* (New York: Sage, 1976), p. 16.
9. Ibid., p. 407.
10. Marvin Sussman, "Activity Patterns of Postparental Couples and the Relationship to Family Continuity," *Marriage and Family Living* 17 (1955): 338–40.
11. Herant A. Katchadourian and Donald Lunde, *Fundamentals of Human Sexuality* (New York: Holt, Rinehart and Winston, 1975), p. 125.
12. Ibid., p. 126.
13. Campbell et al., *Quality*, pp. 412–13.
14. Ibid., p. 407 (chart).
15. Boyd Rollins and Harold Feldman, "Marital Satisfaction over the Family Life Cycle," *Journal of Marriage and the Family* 32 (February 1970): 20–27.
16. Ibid.
17. Cited in Jessie Bernard, *The Future of Marriage* (New York: World, 1972), p. 69.
18. Ibid.
19. Campbell et al., *Quality*, p. 416 (chart).
20. Ibid., p. 416.
21. Ibid., p. 415.
22. Eleanore B. Luckey and Joyce K. Bain, "Children: A Factor in Marital Satisfaction," *Journal of Marriage and the Family* 32 (February 1970): 43–44.
23. Bernard, *Future of Marriage*, p. 48.
24. Rollins and Feldman, "Marital Satisfaction," p. 22.
25. Bernard, *Future of Marriage*, Table 34.
26. Marie Burnett, Ph.D., personal interview.
27. Burnett, personal interview.
28. Burnett, personal interview.
29. Burnett, personal interview.
30. Burnett, personal interview.
31. Bernard, *Future of Marriage*, p. 58.

CHAPTER 4

1. Judith Blake, "Are Babies Consumer Durables?" *Population Studies* 22 (March 1968): 16.
2. *U.S. News & World Report,* February 25, 1980, p. 66.
3. Garrett Hardin, *Birth Control* (New York: Penguin, 1970), p. 26.
4. Blake, "Are Babies Consumer Durables?" pp. 12–18.
5. R. H. Reed and Susan McIntosh, "Costs of Children," in E. R. Morss and R. H. Reeds, eds., *Economic Aspects of Population Change,* Vol. 2 (Washington, D.C.: U.S. Commission on Population Growth and the American Future, 1972), p. 346.
6. Health Insurance Institute, "The Cost of Having a Baby" (Washington, D.C.: Health Insurance Institute, 1978).
7. Rebecca Swain, personal records.
8. New York *Times,* December 18, 1980.
9. Ibid.
10. New York *Times,* February 19, 1981.
11. Reed and McIntosh, "Costs of Children," p. 349.
12. Marianne Kane et al., "Social Rights in Sweden Before School Starts," in Pamela Roby, ed., *Child Care—Who Cares?* (New York: Basic Books, 1973).
13. Reed and McIntosh, "Costs of Children," p. 345.
14. Caroline Bird, *The Two-Paycheck Marriage* (New York: Pocket Books, 1980), pp. 4–5.
15. Cited in N. Newton, *Maternal Emotions* (New York: Paul Hoeber, 1955), p. 28.
16. Blake, "Are Babies Consumer Durables?" pp. 16–17.
17. E. R. Morss and Susan McIntosh Ralph, "Family Life Styles, the Childbearing Decision, and the Influence of Federal Activities: A Quantitative Approach," in E. R. Morss and R. H. Reed, eds., *Economic Aspects of Population Change,* Vol. 2 (Washington, D.C.: U.S. Commission on Population Growth and the American Future, 1972), p. 362.

CHAPTER 5

1. Eli Ginzberg et al., *Life Styles of Educated Women* (New York: Columbia University Press, 1966), pp. 110–11.
2. Cynthia Epstein, *Woman's Place: Options and Limits in Professional*

Careers (Berkeley and Los Angeles: University of California Press, 1970), p. 94.

3. Ibid., p. 151.

4. Lotte Bailyn, "Family Constraints on Women's Work," in Ruth B. Kundsin, ed., *Women & Success: The Anatomy of Achievement* (New York: Morrow, 1974), p. 94.

5. Alice Rossi, "Maternalism, Sexuality, and the New Feminism," in J. Zubin and J. Money, eds., *Contemporary Sexual Behavior* (Baltimore: Johns Hopkins University Press, 1973), p. 153.

6. Ibid., p. 154.

7. Epstein, *Woman's Place*, p. 2.

8. Susan M. Ervin-Tripp, "Women with Ph.D.'s," *Science* 174 (1971): 1281.

9. Epstein, *Woman's Place*, p. 3.

10. Ginzberg et al., *Life Styles*, p. 52.

11. Bailyn, "Family Constraints," p. 97.

12. Ginzberg et al., *Life Styles*, p. 93.

13. Epstein, *Woman's Place*, p. 87.

14. Ginzberg et al., *Life Styles*, pp. 81–82.

15. Epstein, *Woman's Place*, p. 98.

CHAPTER 6

1. Caryl Rivers, Rosalind Barnett, and Grace Baruch, *Beyond Sugar and Spice: How Women Grow, Learn, and Thrive* (New York: Putnam, 1979), p. 303.

2. Margaret Movius, "Voluntary Childlessness—the Ultimate Separation," *The Family Coordinator* 25 (January 1976), 1: 61.

3. Edward Pohlman, *Psychology of Birth Planning* (New York: Schenkman, 1969), p. 115.

4. Carolyn Elliott, "The Superwoman Phenomenon," *Women's Studies Newsletter* VIII, 2 (Spring 1980): 27.

5. Cynthia Epstein, "Bringing Women In: Rewards, Punishments, and the Structure of Achievement," in Ruth B. Kundsin, ed., *Women & Success: The Anatomy of Achievement* (New York: Morrow, 1974), p. 20.

6. Cynthia Epstein, *Woman's Place: Options and Limits in Professional Careers* (Berkeley and Los Angeles: University of California Press, 1970), p. 92.

7. Rivers, Barnett, and Baruch, *Beyond Sugar and Spice*, p. 248.

8. Mariette Nowak, *Eve's Rib: A Revolutionary New View of the Female Sex Roles* (New York: St. Martin's Press, 1980), pp. 147–48.

9. *U.S. News & World Report*, June 16, 1980, p. 57.

10. Ibid.

11. Ibid.

12. New York *Times*, April 15, 1980, p. C2.

13. *U.S. News & World Report*, June 16, 1981, p. 57.

14. Elliott, "The Superwoman Phenomenon," p. 26.

CHAPTER 7

1. Quoted in Carl N. Degler, *At Odds: Women and the Family in America from the Revolution to the Present* (New York: Oxford University Press, 1980), p. 201.

2. Beatrice Forbes-Robertson Hale, *What Women Want: An Interpretation of the Feminist Movement* (New York: Stokes, 1914), p. 276.

3. Quoted in Linda Gordon, *Woman's Body, Woman's Right: A Social History of Birth Control in America* (New York: Grossman, 1976), p. 236.

4. George Devereux, *A Study of Abortion in Primitive Societies*, rev. ed. (New York: International Universities Press, 1976).

5. Gordon, *Woman's Body*, pp. 99–100.

6. Ibid., pp. 111–12.

7. Degler, *At Odds*, p. 204.

8. Quoted in Degler, *At Odds*, p. 205.

9. Ibid.

10. Gordon, *Woman's Body*, p. 143.

11. Anonymous, "By a Childless Wife: Why I Have No Family," *The Independent*, March 23, 1905, p. 654.

12. Ibid.

13. Ibid.

14. Ida Husted Harper, "Small vs. Large Families," *The Independent*, December 26, 1901, pp. 3055–59.

15. Betty Friedan, *The Feminine Mystique* (New York: Norton, 1963).

16. William L. O'Neill, *Everyone Was Brave: A History of Feminism in America* (New York: Quadrangle Books, 1969), p. 353.

CHAPTER 8

1. John Money and Anke A. Ehrhardt, *Man & Woman, Boy & Girl: Differentiation and Dimorphism of Gender Identity from Conception to Maturity* (Baltimore: Johns Hopkins University Press, 1972), pp. 10, 111–12, chap. 6; John Money and Patricia Tucker, *Sexual Signatures* (Boston: Little Brown, 1975), pp. 54–57.

2. Nancy Chodorow, *The Reproduction of Mothering: Psychoanalysis and the Sociology of Gender* (Berkeley and Los Angeles: University of California Press, 1978), p. 26.

3. Marc Bekoff, "Socialization in Mammals with an Emphasis on Non-primates," in Suzanne Chevalier-Skolnikoff and Frank E. Poirer, eds., *Primate Bio-social Development: Biological, Social, and Ecological Determinants* (New York and London: Garland, 1977), p. 606.

4. Ibid.

5. Ann Oakley, *Woman's Work: The Housewife, Past and Present* (New York: Vintage, 1976), p. 200.

6. Chodorow, *Reproduction of Mothering*, p. 27.

7. Money and Ehrhardt, *Man & Woman*, chap. 6.

8. Ibid.

9. Chodorow, *Reproduction of Mothering*, p. 25.

10. Margaret Mead, *Sex and Temperament in Three Primitive Societies* (1935; reprint, New York: Morrow, 1963).

11. Mead, *Sex and Temperament*, p. 39.

12. Linda Marie Fedigan and Laurence Fedigan, "The Social Development of a Handicapped Infant in a Free-living Troop of Japanese Monkeys," in Chevalier-Skolnikoff and Poirer, eds., *Primate Bio-social Development*, p. 209.

13. Nancy A. Nicolson, "A Comparison of Early Behavioral Development on Wild and Captive Chimpanzees," in Chevalier-Skolnikoff and Poirer, eds., *Primate Bio-social Development*, p. 533.

14. Oakley, *Woman's Work*, p. 202.

15. Ibid.; Nicolson, "Comparison of Early Behavioral Development," in Chevalier-Skolnikoff and Poirer, eds., *Primate Bio-social Development*, p. 535.

16. Ann Oakley, *Sex, Gender and Society* (New York: Harper Colophon, 1972), pp. 201–2.

17. Charles F. Westoff and Larry L. Bumpass, *The Later Years of Childbearing* (Princeton: Princeton University Press, 1970), p. 36.

18. George Devereux, *A Study of Abortion in Primitive Societies*, rev. ed. (New York: International Universities Press, 1976).

19. Maria Piers, *Infanticide* (New York: Norton, 1978), pp. 51–52, 54, 68, 123.

20. Jacques Donzelot, *The Policing of Families* (New York: Pantheon, 1979), p. 26.

21. Piers, *Infanticide*, p. 37.

22. Maria Piers, personal interview.

23. Margaret Mead, *Male and Female: A Study of the Sexes in a Changing World* (1949; reprint, New York: Morrow, 1975), p. 233.

CHAPTER 9

1. Sigmund Freud, letter to Marie Bonaparte, in Ernest Jones, *The Life and Work of Sigmund Freud*, Vol. 2 (New York: Basic Books, 1953), p. 421.

2. Barbara Ehrenreich and Dierdre English, *Complaints and Disorders: The Sexual Politics of Sickness*, Pamphlet no. 2 (Old Westbury, N.Y.: Feminist Press, 1973), pp. 43–44.

3. Sigmund Freud, "Female Sexuality," in *The Standard Edition of the Complete Psychological Works of Sigmund Freud*, trans. under general editorship of James Strachey, in collab. with Anna Freud, Vol. XXI (London: Hogarth Press and the Institute of Psychoanalysis, 1961), p. 233.

4. Freud, "Transformation of Puberty," *Standard Ed.*, Vol. VII, p. 219.

5. Marie Bonaparte, *Female Sexuality*, trans. by John Rodker (New York: International Universities Press, 1953), pp. 205–6.

6. Freud, "Female Sexuality," *Standard Ed.*, Vol. XXI, p. 228.

7. Bonaparte, *Female Sexuality*, p. 48.

8. Freud, "Femininity," *New Introductory Lectures on Psychoanalysis*, ed. and trans. by James Strachey (New York: Norton, 1965), p. 119.

9. William H. Masters and Virginia E. Johnson, *Human Sexual Response* (1966; reprint, New York: Bantam, 1980), p. 48.

10. Barbara Seaman and Gideon Seaman, *Women and the Crisis in Sex Hormones* (New York: Bantam, 1978), p. 236.

11. Karen Horney, in Strouse, ed., *Women and Psychoanalysis* (New York: Grossman, 1974), p. 177.

12. Margaret Mead, quoted in Mariette Nowak, *Eve's Rib: A Revolu-*

tionary New View of the Female Sex Roles (New York: St. Martin's
Press, 1980), p. 183.

CHAPTER 10

1. Judith Blake, "Coercive Pronatalism and American Population Policy," in Ellen Peck and Judith Senderowitz, eds., *Pronatalism: The Myth of Mom & Apple Pie* (New York: Crowell, 1974), p. 32.
2. Margaret Mead, *Male and Female: A Study of the Sexes in a Changing World* (1949; reprint, New York: Morrow, 1975), p. 224.
3. Adrienne Rich, *Of Woman Born: Motherhood as Experience and Institution* (New York: Bantam, 1977), p. 275.
4. Ibid.
5. New York *Times,* March 17, 1975.
6. K. H. Mehlan, "Legal Abortions in Roumania," *Journal of Sex Research* 1 (1965): 33.
7. *Population Bulletin,* Vol. 32, No. 1. Population Reference Bureau, Washington, D.C., 1977.
8. Mead, *Male and Female,* pp. 232–33.
9. Leta Hollingworth, "Social Devices for Impelling Women to Bear and Rear Children," in Peck and Senderowitz, eds., *Pronatalism,* p. 18.
10. Jessie Bernard, *The Future of Motherhood* (New York: Penguin, 1975), p. 49.

CHAPTER 11

1. Nancy Chodorow, *The Reproduction of Mothering: Psychoanalysis and the Sociology of Gender* (Berkeley and Los Angeles: University of California Press, 1978).
2. Chodorow, *Reproduction of Mothering,* p. 211.
3. Eleanor Emmons Maccoby and Carol Nagy Jacklin, *The Psychology of Sex Differences* (Stanford: Stanford University Press, 1974).
4. Maccoby and Jacklin, *Sex Differences,* pp. 311–12, 336–38.
5. Ibid., pp. 512–13.
6. Ibid.
7. Ibid., pp. 316–17, 319.
8. Ibid.
9. Ibid., p. 319.
10. Ibid., pp. 321–22.

11. Ibid.
12. Ibid., pp. 325–27.
13. Ibid., p. 326.
14. Malkah T. Notman, "Pregnancy and Abortion: Implications for Career Development in Professional Women," in Ruth B. Kundsin, ed., *Women & Success: The Anatomy of Achievement* (New York: Morrow, 1974), p. 219.

Index

Blake, Judith, 50
"Are Babies Consumer Durables?,"
66
"Coercive Pronatalism and
American Population Policy,"
151
Bonaparte, Marie, 137–39
Breast-feeding, 130
Burnett, Marie, 47–49

Campbell, Angus, 35
Career changes, 76, 77
Careers, 5–9, 88
childlessness and, 18–19, 54–55
children and, 69–87
marriage and, 71–74
maternal ambivalence and, 69–71,
167–69
motherhood and, 19, 41, 74–75,
85–87, 155–67, 166–71
timing birth and, 81–83
working mothers and, 75–81,
96–97. See also Employers
working women and, 75–81
See also Career women; Working
mothers; Working women
Career women, 17, 73
See also Careers
Caretakers, 57–58
See also Day care
Cervical cap, 141–42
Child abuse, 7, 30, 48
Childbearing, 174
postponing, 169–70
Child care, 97–98
superwomen and, 95
tax deduction for, 98
See also Day care
Child costs, 20, 50–68
for college, 63
"everyone can afford a baby"
policy and, 65–68
hospital, 61–62
lost-opportunity costs, 59, 63–65
for material items, 60
premarital conception and, 61

social pressure and, 61
to women, 63–65
Childhoods of childless women,
12–15
Childless couples, voluntarily, 13,
19–22, 54–59
freedom to be, 67
See also Childless marriage
Childless marriage, 28–49
crisis of children and, 29–33
financial changes and, 34–36
happiness of, 41–45, 49
interpersonal changes and, 38–41
sexual changes and, 36–38
See also Childless couples
Childless men, 46
Childlessness, 101–2, 157
cultural pressure and, 148–58
early roots of, 108–10
elite class and, 52–59
feminists and, 108–12
marriage and, 46–47
maternal ambivalence and, 170–71
politics of, 101–17, 151–55
psychological view of, 11
self-image and, 25–27
socialization of, 26
stigma of, 24–25
women's movement and, 113–17
Childless widow, 4–5
Childless women, voluntarily, 3–4,
8–9, 11, 13–14, 146
careers and, 18–19, 69
care for younger siblings by, 15
childhoods of, 12–15
children and, 22–24
creativity and, 86–87
cultural pressure and, 155–56
data on, 10
as deviants, 74, 121
employers and, 84–85
family position of, 15–16
femininity of, 26, 143
feminism and, 102, 104–8
freedom to be, 67
in Freudian theory, 137
happiness of, 41–45